QUESTIONS 1
ISLAM
CAN'T ANSWER
VOLUME ONE

WRITTEN BY
J.K SHEINDLIN

For all information about this author, visit:
www.jksheindlin.com

Copyright © 2017 by J.K Sheindlin

All rights reserved. No part of this publication may be reproduced, distributed or transmitted, in any form or by any means, electronic, mechanical, including photocopying, recording, or any information storage and retrieval system, without written permission from the publisher, except by a reviewer who wishes to quote brief passages in relation to a critical article and review written for inclusion in a magazine, newspaper, or broadcast.

ABOUT THE AUTHOR

J.K Sheindlin is the author of the controversial #1 international bestseller 'The People vs Muhammad' book series. Sheindlin is a passionate contributor to the fight against injustice and the growing threat of universal censorship. The author has spent years researching the true origins of Islam and has fervently documented the rise of Islamization in western countries. J.K wishes to extend an invitation of reason and common sense to any group who seem incapable of opening their eyes to the truth, or debating intelligently without violent retaliation.

This book is dedicated to those whom the system has failed, to the millions who have fallen through the cracks, and to the multitudes who have been silenced by those who will soon kneel before God and confess that HE is Lord. To the meek who shall inherit the world, who have been vilified by the cowardly who dare not ask both the right and wrong questions. I stand with you.

Truth is the ultimate comforter,
vindicator of the righteous and unjustly silenced.

CONTENTS

FOREWORD	8
WHY DID I WRITE THIS BOOK SERIES?	11
DANGEROUS QUESTIONS	14
REFERENCES AND BIBLIOGRAPHY	20

QUESTIONS ABOUT ISLAM AND THE QURAN

WHY ARE ISLAMIC COUNTRIES ALWAYS ECONOMICALLY STAGNANT AND CULTURALLY RETROGRADE? — 22

A FAILED NATION AND AN ABSENT GOD	23
THE MIDDLE-CHILD OF HISTORY	26
OIL EXPORTS AND FOREIGN AID	30
ISLAM'S ABYSMAL IQ RATING	37
ISRAEL AND THE JEWS - THE MUSLIM BUGBEAR	40
THE VOICE OF REASON	42
AN ECHO FROM THE PAST	47

WHY ARE MORE WOMEN GOING TO HELL THAN MEN, ACCORDING TO MUHAMMAD? 49

AN INSUFFICIENT NUMBER OF PRAYERS	52
STUPID PEOPLE DON'T GO TO HEAVEN?	55
A MAN MADE RELIGION	59
PRIDE COMES BEFORE THE FALL	60

WHY IS THERE NO SALVATION IN ISLAM? — 63

DON'T PEE ON YOUR SHOES, YOU'LL GO TO HELL	64
JIHAD	66
MUHAMMAD IS IN HELL	69
I'LL PAY WITH CHRISTIAN BLOOD	71
ANYONE WANT TO PLAY A GAME OF LIMBO?	73
PBUH?	75

IF SHARIA IS GOD'S LAW, WHY DOES IT FAIL EVERYONE?   78

HERE COME THE MUSLIMS	78
MUSLIM INFERIORITY COMPLEX	80
ALLAH'S PERFECT LAW?	81
WOE TO THE MUSLIM WOMAN	82
THANKS ALLAH, FOR RUINING MY LIFE	85
HOMOSEXUAL MUSLIMS DON'T EXIST?	86
WHO HAS THE CORRECT ANSWER?	88
SHARIA BANKING FAILS THE WORLD ENTIRE	89
LET'S BLAME THE WEST	90

WHY IS THERE NO PROOF THAT MUHAMMAD EXISTED?   92

NO DNA EVIDENCE	94
MR. IBN ABDULLAH?	96
THE FORGOTTEN PROPHET	98
THE MUSLIM CHAUCER	99
DON'T TAKE MY PICTURE!	101
THE MAN WHO WASN'T THERE	104

WHY IS THERE NO PROOF THAT ISLAM EXISTED BEFORE MUHAMMAD'S BIRTH?   106

NO CONVERTS, ONLY REVERTS	107
CONVENIENT DISAPPEARANCE OF THE ANCIENT ISLAMIC WORLD	108
THE NIGHT JOURNEY	111
NO RECORD OF ISLAM OUTSIDE OF ARABIA	113
WHERE'S ADAM'S REMAINS?	115
THE SCAPEGOAT	117
THE PALESTINIAN MYTH	119
HALLMARKS OF A CULT	121

WHY IS ISLAM NEVER MENTIONED IN THE BIBLE? — 123

THE BIBLE IS CORRUPT?	124
HAS ANYONE SEEN THE INJEEL?	128
THE HELPER?	133
A PROPHET WHO FULFILLED NO PROPHECIES	135
THE MECCA PARADOX	139
A FLAWED RELIGION FOR A FLAWED PROPHET	141

WHY IS THERE NO PROOF MECCA EXISTED IN ANCIENT TIMES? — 143

THE MECCAN TRINITY PARADOX	144
ARCHAEOLOGICALLY AND LOGICALLY UNSOUND	146
WHICH KA'ABA IS IT, MUHAMMAD?	147
BACA OR MACORABA?	149
A HISTORICAL TRADING HUB?	151
THE KHADIJA PARADOX	153
AN EMPTY SHOP	154
WHY DOES MECCA EXIST TODAY?	155
ANY MECCA WILL DO	156
IF THE QURAN IS INCORRUPTIBLE, WHY WERE THE EARLY COPIES DESTROYED?	**159**
THE QURAN HAS REMAINED UNCHANGED?	161
AN EMBARRASSING FIASCO	163
WHEN IN DOUBT, BURN IT?	165
ONLY PROPHETS CAN CERTIFY THE QURAN	167
AN INCOHERENT BOOK	169
UNDISCIPLINED DISCIPLES	174
WHAT WAS WRITTEN IN THE ORIGINAL QURAN?	176
WHEN WAS ISLAM NEVER AN EXTREMIST RELIGION?	**177**

THE MUSLIM PROPAGANDA	179
MY JIHAD?	179
AN EXTREMIST RELIGION	180
IMMODERATE ISLAM	183
THE GREAT MUSLIM IMPOSITION	185
FANATICAL AND FATALISTIC	187
THE APARTHEID RELIGION	190
ISLAM IS ISLAM - A GENOCIDAL CULT	194

FOREWORD

First and foremost, I strongly urge anyone who has bought this book to also acquire a copy of my first critically acclaimed publication, 'The People vs Muhammad'. This contentious and controversial book series has now become an international bestseller, and is widely considered as the new gold standard in explaining Islam, and most importantly, *exposing* Muhammad himself.

Due to the polarising nature of my first book, 'The People vs Muhammad - Psychological Analysis', it has been set to be banned and censored by the Canadian Federation of Library Associations. At the same time, and not surprisingly, it has been banned in the Arab states, and now on Amazon India. Nonetheless, despite the echelon's desperate attempts to silence the truth, the book series remains on the international bestseller lists in 'Religious studies' and 'Religion, State and Politics':

#1 in USA
#1 in UK
#1 in Canada
#1 in Germany

To verify these records, you can visit my website and watch the video '5 star reviews'.

The critically acclaimed success of the book series is attributed to the unprecedented work I pioneered in psychologically analysing Muhammad, which is the first time in history anyone has truly delved deep into the man's psyche, his sexual habits, and psychopathy. Perhaps the most startling revelation, is the fact that Muhammad most probably was afflicted with syphilis, which in turn evolved into neurosyphilis, finally manifesting into paranoid schizophrenia. It is from this sexually transmitted disease which undoubtedly gave birth to Islam, and its eccentric tenets. In my first book, I also divulged to the public the sordid details of what Muslims purport to be 'the most perfect human being'; these being Muhammad's extensive history of engaging in pedophilia, prostitution, homosexuality and necrophilia. I made numerous academic references to prove my case - none have been able to refute the truth.

'The People vs Muhammad' is the first book series in history which has called for the posthumous prosecution of the founder of Islam, for crimes against humanity. While the trial still continues, my new book series *'Questions that Islam can't answer'* will prove to be an invaluable tool in waking up Muslims to the truth. I guarantee that no Muhammadan will be able to answer the questions found within this book, nor comprehend how they could have been deceived their entire life. And at the same time, the contents of this series will serve to be a testing tool for Muslims who willingly refuse to accept the truth, and wilfully continue to engage in the same depraved acts as their master.

Understandably so, most critics of Islam dare not venture too close to the flames, and will *never* criticise the *founder* in fear of reprisal. I believe that the people deserve better. For far too long, Islam has wiped its feet on our faces and hijacked the role of moral superiority. I intend to end this growing trend of western capitulation, and fight back with the truth.

On a final note, I have also produced a documentary series which will be available on DVD. The multipart movie series will reveal classified intelligence about Islam's insidious and steady takeover of the west, and how our leaders have capitulated to the cult for financial profit. The movie series will be released soon, and is guaranteed to shake the foundations of our society. For more information, please visit my website: www.jksheindlin.com

WHY DID I WRITE THIS BOOK SERIES?

For anyone who has read my first book, they will know my reputation for unflinchingly exposing hypocrisy, lies and spiritual fraudulence. I do not believe that anything beneficial can be gained from imbibing falsehoods, or complicity allowing lies to fester in our society.

Islam is the mother of all lies. It's a disjointed, incoherent narrative, albeit certainly concise regarding its murderous ideology. It is immensely insecure of its own origins, and thus projects its frustrations at the world. To put it simply, Muslims hate questions. Moreover *questions* that ultimately embarrasses their faith, or those which they cannot answer. To a Muslim, Islam is allegedly perfect, and without inquiry.

I wrote this book series for the layman, and as a supplementary companion for 'The People vs Muhammad' series. Understandably, while my first book series is quite overwhelming with academic sources, this series was written to be an easy read, and a handy companion in the fight against Islam. I have tried to make each chapter as concise as possible without bloviating incessantly with copious amounts of references. Likewise, I believe that the logical arguments provided within are profound enough to stump the worst Muslim firebrand.

Throughout this series, I will make references to 'Islam' or the 'Ummah', and thus I intend to group the entire ideology and its adherents together as one people; *Muhammadans* who are under the spell of their prophet. Likewise, there will be no room for ambiguity, especially when I refer to the Quran, the Hadith and Tafsir in my quest for truth.

As we have all become aware of by now, Muslims are excessively and disturbingly proud of their religion, and wholeheartedly believe that Islam and Muhammad have the answers for everything unanswerable. As you've most probably heard many times before from Muslims, *"Islam is the solution for mankind's problems."* And by that regard, they truly believe that Muhammad is allegedly the most *perfect* man who ever lived. For those who know me personally, I take such arrogant statements as a direct challenge to be disproved and dissected. It's who I am, and I make no apologies for it.

I wrote this series because many Muslims don't even know their own religion. Most have never read the chronicles of Muhammad, not even the entire Quran. But all believe that they have complete knowledge of Islam, more so than a filthy kuffir (unbeliever) such as myself. Through the eyes of a Muslim, no infidel could possibly produce anything of value. Ergo, books such as these are always regarded by Muslims as propaganda, lies, or a mendacious subversion of the faith. Yet I've always maintained that Muslims wouldn't know the difference between the Islamic texts and their own phone book. Most Arabs are illiterate and rely solely on oral tradition. However, after Muslims migrate to the west, the fact that books such as these exist, is no doubt a shock to their system. For a Muslim, it is incomprehensible how mankind could even question Muhammad. Without reading so much as a page of my books, the contents within are flippantly disregarded as heresy. In truth, the overwhelming majority of Muslims are only culturally attached to Islam, and follow tradition primarily. Sadly, they are entirely oblivious to the truth that remains within the tomes of their own Islamic scripture. And thus, they are pawns in Muhammad's sick system; akin to twigs floating on top of a violently flowing stream, soon to be released into an ocean of peril.

Thus, I wrote this series to test their allegedly vast knowledge of Islam. As I've been told innumerably by Muslims with condescending scorn, *"You know nothing about Islam, you're not a Muslim. Only a Muslim can understand true Islam."* And so, the tables have turned. Instead of myself dictating to the Ummah, the burden of proof is now bestowed upon them. If Islam is *the truth*, then they will be able to answer these simple questions with ease. If not, then they must concede that Islam is still found wanting, and cannot answer life's mysteries or the inane, illogical teachings dictated by Muhammad.

I implore the reader to use common sense in broaching the included topics in this book with any Muslim. I guarantee that no true Muhammadan will be able to answer these questions completely without typically imploding, or decrying them as 'hate speech!'

Tread carefully.

DANGEROUS QUESTIONS

All ideas begin with questions. Since the dawn of time, civilisations which have come and gone, all based their creed, faith and reason, on the fundamental premise of self-examination. We're all inquisitive by nature, at least for the majority who haven't been indoctrinated into a political cult. It's normal for any rationally minded person to question the world they live in, the 'truth', the origin of life and the hereafter.

How would we know what is right or wrong if we did not *question?* It is from rigorous investigations into the world we know, that we have developed the power of *reason*. Sadly, Islam somehow considers itself exempt from inquiry and the overall concept of reasoning. Equally so, *conscience* in Islam is alien, as Muhammad himself removed moral standards and self-awareness from his followers. In fact, the Quran states that a Muslim should not question the teachings of Muhammad, no matter how absurd or disturbing they are, and must always disable his or her brain…

> "O you who have believed, do not ask about things which, if they are shown to you, will distress you."
> Quran 5:101

Without 'conscience', a Muslim simply acts upon instinct, predetermined by set parameters within their psychological construct - this being comprised of the fundamentals of Sharia law. A true follower of the cult would unquestionably cut off an infidel's head without batting an eye, or fatally maim their daughter over suggestions of apostasy.

Islam believes it is the pinnacle of morality, without question. It considers barbarity tantamount to civility, compassion as a weakness, and rationality akin to apostasy. In truth, Islam flips the world upside down. What is good becomes evil, and evil becomes good. This trend of lunacy has continued unabated ever since the founding fathers of Islam gave up their free will for the cult. Not once in the last 1400 years, has any Muslim ever attempted to change the fundamental tenets set by Muhammad. This has been their journey, which has ultimately equated to their own undoing.

But the origin of my story is far removed from a Muslim's compulsion to adhere to religious dogma. As the reader might be aware, I have remained exceptionally discreet about my identity. However, I will reveal one detail of how I began my study into Islam. What had turned into a fleeting curiosity over religion, set me on a path to ascertain the truth. The more I read of the Quran and the Hadith, it became bluntly apparent that something was definitely rotten about Islam's core. Whether it was regarding Muhammad's penchant for raping little children, the incestuous relationship with his aunt, or his rampant misogyny - it was obvious that the man was certainly a very messed up individual. And thus, I found a way in to cross-examine Muslims about their beliefs.

For many years, I began asking Muslims all the *wrong* questions on internet forums, blogs, online chat rooms, and at the local mosque. Not out of malice or jest, but to see if the alleged infallible religion could explain the fallibility of their prophet. At the time, I was quite surprised that all questions were rebuked as provocation without warrant, despite the charges axiomatically presenting themselves. Consequently, Muslims censored my questions without even taking the time to answer them with logic - simply because there is no *logic* in

Islam. Naturally, they were only emulating their prophet; a man who was not at all fond of being questioned. In fact, Muhammad despised the inquisitive. Being the narcissist that he was, the 'prophet' only tolerated persistent queries up until the point where he would callously, and impulsively behead who he deemed insubordinate. The line between reasoning and delinquency was only razor thin.

An example of this behaviour is demonstrated in my first book, of which I divulged a particular Islamic tradition where an ardent follower of the cult was beheaded simply for standing his ground against the biased decision set by Muhammad. But traditions such as these are not obscure. For anyone who would take a moment to read a few chapters of the Sirat (biography) of Muhammad, it is plainly evident that the man slowly removed the inherent nature of reasoning from his people, until they were completely mentally enslaved, devoid of conscience.

However, now acting as a journalist myself, I am tasked with questioning *everything*. Good journalism comes from asking questions that no-one dare broach. Within this book, I have tried to be objective as possible, and posed the primary questions which undoubtedly are the flaws in Islam's allegedly *flawless* ideology. Ironically, if Islam was truly infallible, the following questions would not exist.

I was once told that there is no such thing as a stupid question. And while that may be the case, there is certainly an element of danger in not just asking the right questions, but instead what is politically incorrect. In today's climate, it is the nature of investigation which has become the most effective weapon in fighting corruption and political blindness. Those who are guilty of concealing the truth are always threatened by the mere whisper of conjecture.

Make no mistake, we are in the fight of our lives. The less we tackle the problem that is Islam, the worst off we'll be. The liberal establishment is openly sharing an incestuous relationship with Islam, based on the common principles of subterfuge, cultural marxism and temporal pacifism. It's apparent today that many people, mostly liberals and Muslims, would rather attack my personal character than admit to the truth. Muslims specifically, invariably rely on conspiracy theories, accusations of 'Zionism', or just plainly dissemble to avoid the heat. Liberals are only concerned with questioning my politics to cover up their failure in recognising the threat that is Islam.

Both have attacked my credibility, my style of writing, my objectivity, and obfuscated with cover stories of Islamic fables to embellish the gory details of Muhammad's life. And through the haze of contention, the persistent embittered polemics, the childish liberal retorts, and diversionary tactics, they bank on the chance that the truth might actually get lost in the chaos. And in most cases, it does. Muslims are masters of deceptive apologetics when it comes to the truth. And when cornered with the condemning facts, they will kick and scream, harass, denigrate, and in the end we seldom even remember what the issue was about. But let's get down to brass tacks. We are being assaulted from all sides. No longer can we even seek solace and wisdom from the church, which once was the stronghold of Christendom. Instead, many parishes have given in to the seducing mantras of *false peace* in exchange for our sovereignty. It is pastors such as Rick Warren who promulgate the insidious hybridisation known as 'Chrislam', and more recently, the Catholic church which has completely submitted to the faith.

> *"Muslim terrorism does not exist.* They do not exist" - Pope Francis 2017

Equally so…

> "*Muslim* terrorist. That wording is wrong. Any person who wants to indulge in violence is no longer a genuine Muslim, because it is a Muslim teaching that once you are involved in bloodshed, actually you are no longer a genuine practitioner of Islam."
> The Dalai Lama

But according to Muhammad…

> "Those who believe fight in the cause of Allah"
> Quran 4:76

> "They but wish that ye should reject Faith, as they do, and thus be on the same footing (as they): But take not friends from their ranks until they flee in the way of Allah (From what is forbidden). But if they turn renegades, seize them and slay them wherever ye find them; and (in any case) take no friends or helpers from their ranks."
> Quran 4:89

> "And kill them wherever you find them, and turn them out from where they have turned you out.

> And Al-Fitnah [disbelief or unrest] is worse than killing... fight them until there is no more Fitnah [disbelief and worshipping of others along with Allah] and worship is for Allah alone."
> Quran 2:191-193

These are perilous times. The fact that you're reading this book, makes you yourself a journalist, and a champion of democracy. Cherish the gift of reason while you can. While freedom is a God-given right, in reality it is not guaranteed. We have to fight for it, and defend it at all costs.

Sadly, we have become a nation of appeasement, where our leaders have transformed overnight into snivelling lackeys, bowing before a dictatorial, fascist oil-rich nation, and have become infatuated with the prospect of destroying the legacy of their civilization through political correctness to line their own pockets. We deserve better. We have fought too hard and for too long to let our civilization be destroyed by a barbaric, insidious, political doctrine, which has no business in our God given lands. Our strength and resolve is founded in the eternal promise of God's given right to freedom, and the accompanying privilege of reason. For what is man without reason, but merely animals.

Your quest has begun.

REFERENCES AND BIBLIOGRAPHY

For the reader's benefit, I have included a number of important references to give this book some background and context regarding the Islamic narrative, of which I will refer to as the 'Islamic texts' and their 'traditions'. While some of these stories are included in the Quran and Hadith codex, the majority are told in greater chronological detail in the following books:

Biography of Muhammad by Ibn Ishaq
Kitab al-Tarikh wa al-Maghazi by al-Waqidi
Kitab Al-Tabaqat Al-Kabir by Ibn Sa'd
The History of al-Tabari
The Tafsir and The Life of the Prophet Muhammad by Ibn Kathir

I have listed these books so that there will be no ambiguity, as the reader can easily check these sources to verify my statements. Some of the traditions I will discuss are so inane and incredulous that I'm sure many will believe that I'm fabricating these legends. But believe me, the Islamic fables are all verifiable within the aforementioned books. Most traditions are cross-referential, as each work is derivative of the last it was built on. Most of these books are available to read online at various Islamic libraries. Likewise, the corresponding traditions can be easily found via a quick internet search, which will reveal the source.

QUESTIONS ABOUT ISLAM AND THE QURAN

"Do not go where the path may lead; go instead where there is no path and leave a trail."
- *Ralph Waldo Emerson*

WHY ARE ISLAMIC COUNTRIES ALWAYS ECONOMICALLY STAGNANT AND CULTURALLY RETROGRADE?

For what is absolutely clear and irrefutable, the Islamic nation has remained in a consistent state of stagnation for the last millennia. Undeniably, the west has historically surpassed the Islamic middle-east in terms of sociology, economy, technology, and scientific discovery. This inescapable fact is perhaps the biggest bugbear for the Islamic nation, which boldly, and arrogantly claims superiority above all peoples. According to Islam, and more specifically its 'holy' book *the Quran*, Muslims have been personally selected by the most powerful and omniscient force in the universe, Allah, to be the most evolved, perfect, unparalleled and the 'best of all peoples'.

> "You are the best of peoples, evolved for mankind, enjoining what is right, forbidding what is wrong, and believing in Allah. If only the People of the Book had faith, it were best for them: among them are some who have faith, but most of them are perverted transgressors."
> Quran 3:110

This Quranic verse is the linchpin in Islam which bolsters Muslim arrogance, the Islamic supremacist complex, and impinges on their natural human progression. Because of the west's invaluable ingenuity in technology and science, it has indirectly embarrassed Islam, leaving it by the wayside as some long forgotten Bedouin cult that refused to evolve.

Of course, this simple fact is intolerable for the common Muhammadan, and thus Muslims must reject the west has a heretical nation steeped in the *haram* (forbidden). *"It is they who are wrong! We have evolved, as Allah has ordained"*, a Muslim will protest. But how could any Muslim possibly hold a straight face when purporting such drivel, especially when the west, its adversary, has unquestionably superseded the Islamic nation for hundreds of years? The idea that a Muslim must play *catch-up* with the west is an abominable concept, worth condemnation by Allah himself. For any Muslim to accept failure, to acknowledge their substandard sociological status in this great world, is primarily the catalyst for the perpetually self-destructive, petulant, powder-keg that is the middle-east.

Surely, in the mind of a Muslim, it is the infidels who are actually backwards and retrograde. Sadly, the aforementioned Quran verse - conceited, presumptuous, and not written by any god, but dictated by a simple, illiterate and insecure dwarf - has irreversibly prevented Islam from ever moving out of the dark ages. The verse itself, among hundreds of other boastful proclamations, has set the tone for the *entire* Quran; a manuscript underpinned by apartheid values, false bravado and deception.

A FAILED NATION AND AN ABSENT GOD

Undeniably, as Muslims have failed in almost every facet of civilization, their actions have directly proven their god to be nothing but a charlatan and a fraudulent soothsayer. For if Allah truly was an omniscient god, he would have foreseen the *car crash* that is Islam thousands of years before creation, thus moving the cup of dignity to a more suitable candidate worthy of a title 'the best of all peoples'. This riddle itself is somewhat of a paradox, more so for any Muslim who has internalised the position of eternal pride. Had Allah been the true god, real in every way, Muslims would historically and contemporarily be known as successful, civilized and second to none. They're not. Ergo, this paradoxical argument inevitably draws a conclusion which no Muslim would ever accept - Allah could not exist.

While I'm sure many will rebuke this book as nothing but a 'rant', conjecture, and a slander piece, I prefer to use logic and the raw facts to augment my claim. Statistically speaking, the Islamic nation is abysmally substandard on almost every educational world index. In terms of education and literacy, the Muslim Arab states ranked considerably and persistently lower than its western counterparts, in some areas dropping as low as 40% under the west's average. Considering that the west itself is seeing its own education levels in decline, this also screams volumes about Islam's claim to superiority, and leaves much to be desired. These aren't my own contentions. The analytics were published by none other than the United Nations Human development report; human development data 1990-2015.

In fact, the widely respected Pew Research Centre's study about religion and education in 2016, concluded that the Muslim nation has the lowest level of education in the world after Hindus. It's confronting and staggering to find that 36% of the Muslim world have little to absolutely no formal education or training. Which itself lends to the problem that is Islamic terrorism - no hope or future will in turn create a violent vacuum, mired in destruction, self-pity, self-loathing, where Muslims will project their frustrations on their perceived 'oppressors', the west. Consequently, due to the lack of opportunities within these vacuums, Muslims will fervently cling to the Quran as their only hope of salvation. The irony is that their book has destroyed their future, placing them in an untenable position of self-questioning: *Reject Islam and be saved, or defend the prophet and remain in the darkness.* The latter is invariably the self-delusional path that the Islamic nation embarks upon, and thus the cycle of violence will continue unabated until the sun stops rising.

While Muslims may posit that Turkey and Iran demonstrate significantly higher levels of education to its Arab counterparts, one must remember that Turkey is in fact heavily influenced by the west, namely Europe. In fact, if Ataturk himself had not cast off the shackles of Islamic fundamentalism 94 years ago, the shadow of the Ottoman empire would have further pushed Turkish Muslims deeper down to the usual regressive path. It was the father of Turkey who recognised the fundamental flaws in Islamic theocratic impositions which was choking the populous from ever progressing to Europe's standards. Historically speaking, the Ottoman empire might at one point had been a dominant power, thriving in culture, academia and scientific discovery, but it was the Quran and Muhammadism which inevitably chained them to the past.

Iran itself was once a thriving western influenced nation, before the Islamic revolution completely destroyed her, relegating the Persians to the bottom of the international pile. Today, the nation is more hell-bent on nuclear ambitions through their desire to usher in an Islamic messiah by acts of terror, than actually investing in their future. Of course, what nation needs to worry about their future when they're mandated to self-destruct, to force the advent of a fabled Muslim messiah? Thus their Islamic-influenced appetite for destruction has once again prevented them from actually creating regional stability, manufacturing produce, achieving academic prowess or technological advancement. Like many other failed Islamic nations, it is the Quran itself which has shackled Iranians to blind zealotry, and chartered its own course into annihilation. Not surprisingly, this can be said for the majority of Muslim nations which inherently have a propensity to self-harm, all in the name of their prophet. The truth is that not only is Islam a stagnant nation, it is a stagnant ideology, incapable of change or achievement.

THE MIDDLE-CHILD OF HISTORY

Unquestionably, the Muslim nation fits the typical characterisation of the psychologically classified middle-child syndrome; petulant, unable to practice diplomacy, loud and rambunctious, rebellious, coddled by authority, attention-seeking, living off handed-down items, the list goes on. For anyone to doubt these words, let's look at the facts. Islam is not an ancient religion. In fact, it is perhaps one of the newest faiths created. But what cannot be denied is that the Islamic nation fits between the ancient, and the modern. In truth, the Muslim Ummah has struggled to reconcile its faith with both sides of history. Muhammad's inane pontifications undoubtedly conflicted with archaeology, and his asinine revelations and example prohibited Muslims from catching up with the contemporary. Ladies and gentlemen, this only proves that Islam is *the* middle-child of history.

How can Muslims deny this fact when Muhammad himself prohibited innovation and advancement by way of revelation. The Islamic term "Bi'dah", meaning 'innovation', is strictly forbidden by Allah. While the meaning is usually attributed to religious thought, it undoubtedly branches out to all facets of Islamic life, including technology, social politics, and progression.

Allah's Messenger said, "If somebody innovates something which is not in harmony with the principles of our religion, that thing is rejected."
Sahih Bukhari 3:49:861

"The Messenger of Allah said: 'Allah refuses to accept the good deeds of one who follows innovation until he gives up that innovation.'"
Sunan Ibn Majah 1:1:50

The Messenger of Allah said: "Whoever innovates something in this matter of ours (i.e. Islam) that is not part of it, will have it rejected."
Sunan Ibn Majah 1:1:14

It is from these verses which have locked the cult into a state of perpetual regression for over a millennia. Still not convinced that Islam is perhaps the most retrograde force on this planet? Let us consider the facts. Ask the following questions to anyone on the street…

How many Ivy league Muslim colleges can you name?
How many Muslim academics can you think of?
When was the last time you used Islamic medicine?
When was the last time the Muslim world invented anything of value?
How is the world better from Islamic innovation?
Can you name one Muslim nobel peace winner who was bestowed the award for scientific discovery?

I guarantee that no Muslim could answer any of these queries without running to his Imam for guidance, all within the confines of a Muslim 'safe space'. And yet, Muslims still propagate the fallacious notion that Islam is, and always played a significant role in history's progression. We all still have vivid memories of former President Obama oozing over Egyptian Muslims at Al-Azhar University during his 'apology tour'. Who can forget Obama's hollow proclamations, alleging that Islam "has always been a part of America's story." The whopper of platitudes resonated throughout the world when Barry awkwardly stated,

"Innovation in Muslim communities... developed our understanding of how disease spreads and how it can be healed. Islamic culture has given us majestic arches and soaring spires; timeless poetry and cherished music... And throughout history, Islam has demonstrated through words and deeds the possibilities of religious tolerance and racial equality."

Undoubtedly, from the saccharin rhetoric emanating from Obama's lips, it was clear that the man had drank the cool-aid. Firstly, it was Muhammad himself who said that infectious diseases do not exist. Secondly, Islam has no exclusive rights over architecture in the form of arches and spires. One needs to remind the man of the accomplishments achieved by the ancient Romans, the Greeks and Persians. The last time I checked, no Islamic empire built the Pyramids, the Colosseum, the Pantheon, the Acropolis, the Aqueduct, or the hanging gardens of Babylon. Muslims can't deny that the Ottoman empire's achievements were reflections of ancient Europe's own cultural influences. There's no secret why the Ottoman's surpassed their Arab counterparts; the empire was *Eurocentric*, not Arab-centric.

Likewise, perhaps Obama forgot that Muhammad strictly forbade music and poetry...

"Narrated Aisha: Abu Bakr came to my house while two small Ansari girls were singing beside me the stories of the Ansar concerning the Day of Buath. And they were not singers. Abu Bakr said protestingly, "Musical instruments of Satan in the house of Allah's Apostle !" It happened on the 'Id day and Allah's Apostle said, "O Abu Bakr! There is an 'Id for every nation and this is our 'Id."
Sahih Bukhari 2:15:72

And...

"Abu Sa`id Khudri reported: We were going with Allah's Messenger (may peace be upon him). As we reached the place (known as) Arj there met (us) a poet who had been reciting poetry. Thereupon Allah's Messenger (may peace be upon him) said: Catch the satan or detain the satan, for filling the belly of a man with pus is better than stuffing his brain with poetry."
Sahih Muslim 28:5611

Lastly, the topic of religious tolerance and racial equality were concepts Muhammad vehemently rebuked. It was Muhammad who enforced strict Sharia above all faiths, and claimed that Islam is an Arab religion. This is the reason why translated Qurans are always entitled 'the meaning of the Quran'; to convert the book into a foreign language is borderline *haram*. Islamic prayers must only be in *Arabic*, as Allah can only understand this language alone. Thus it also explains why Chinese, Pakistani, Indonesian and western Muslims wear 7th century Arab attire.

For a President to utter such rubbish about Islam's alleged 'religious tolerance and racial equality', it was a blatant and desperate act of reaching, which casted further scrutiny on the religion's obvious state of retroactivity and inadequacy. While these facts are indeed insulting to political correctness, the confounding truth is that the Muslim nation of late has survived solely on two factors…

OIL EXPORTS AND FOREIGN AID

Saudi oil is by far the binding glue which has precariously kept the Arabian peninsular in a state of economic-stability. But alas, as history has proven once again, if the west had not intervened, the Saudi states would not be far removed from the Bedouin days of past. Let's face it, the Arab tribes of the bygone era wouldn't know an oil drill from a cappuccino machine. Alas, the trillions of the dollars pouring into the Islamic nation is not due to Muslim ingenuity. Au contraire! It was the *Americans* who discovered commercial quantities of oil at the Damman well. The rest is, as they say, history. But again, it is this inconvenient truth which not only proves that Muslims are incapable of manufacturing goods, but also sourcing their own resources.

It is undeniable that this historical fact proves once again that Muhammad was a false prophet. After all, considering his alleged clairvoyance and unprecedented powers, surely he could have seen the ocean of oil under his feet. But throughout the Hadith and even the Quran, there is no mention of this valuable commodity. Neither is there any prophecy mentioning the world's dependency on the resource. It's ironic that 'the Bible', a book which Muslims claim is corrupted, reveals in detail the end-times geopolitical climate and the world's over dependency on *Arab* oil.

And while oil-starved Muslim nations remain in a state of perpetual stagnation, Saudi Arabia, the Emirates, and the Qatari landscape, are decorated and furnished with glass superstructures, mega malls, hotels and commercial hubs, all soaring into the desert sky - ironically, all engineered by American and European contractors. Even after all these years, these Muslim nations have failed to invest their riches in academics and are still heavily reliant on the west for engineering innovation.

To add insult to injury, these hi-tech oasis's were not built by Muslim hands, but on the backs of slave labour from Sri Lanka, India and other impoverished nations. In fact, the trend of forced labour came under the international watchdog's spotlight after mass reports of deprivation of liberty and torture. Sri Lankan workers were forbidden from returning home after Arab companies refused to return their passports. At the same time, employees were made to work overtime in 40°C heat, while supervisors prohibited scheduled breaks and consumption of water. Perhaps Obama was either ignorant of this embarrassing debacle, or deliberately concealed the facts when he stated that Islam has a history of "racial equality." Understandably, the man would have to turn a blind eye to these abuses, especially when bending over to kiss the former Saudi king's right hand. Actions always speak louder than words. Of course, slave labour in Islam is not a nascent concept, but an age old and respected tradition. According to Muhammad, slavery is ordained by Allah:

> "And inflict the prescribed punishment on those whom your right hands possess (i.e. slaves)."
> Sunan Abu Dawud 38:4458

For the Muslim nations which are still living in the dark ages, foreign aid is the only means to sustain their existence. Historically, for reasons I will never understand, America has acted beyond the boundaries of generosity to the point of cultural suicide. The great nation has persistently donated billions of dollars to Islamic countries, more so to those who have verbalised their intent to bring down the west, specifically their benefactor.

For decades, Pakistan has been supported by every dollar given by the American taxpayer. The country which surreptitiously aided and housed Osama bin Laden, is set to receive over $742 million in 2017. Quite a handsome sum for an indolent and ineffective country which unashamedly, and rampantly persecutes Christians. Unquestionably, it is America's coddling of these rogue states which sends mix signals, and rings the virtual dinner bell for all to besiege her. How can any rival respect their adversary, when their opponent willingly throws down their arms? This has been the west's long-standing flaw which has witnessed the steady demise of its once sovereign civilization.

The ongoing list of beneficiaries under the United States' foreign aid program is staggering. Not surprisingly, 99% of donations are to oil-rich countries, or states with ties to Muslim oil. Of course, these 'gratuity' donations are to grease the wheels of dependency on oil, lest we revert back to horse and cart. The Arab states know this, and are exploiting their power to the full extent. It also explains why our western leaders are lauding over Muslims, and bending over backwards to donate to countries which are terrorist factories. To keep the oil flowing, the west must keep up the appearance of a subordinate civilization to a despotic Islamic regime; always putting their guests first before their own citizens. But I'm digressing. If anyone is to doubt the actual amount of our tax paying money going to Muslim countries, let us check the facts.

In 2017, the United States is set to donate over $41 billion in foreign aid; seven out of the top ten are Muslim countries. The following list is only a fraction of what has been allocated through foreign aid:

Country: Jordan
Amount: set to receive $1 billion in foreign aid in 2017
A somewhat peaceful Muslim nation, yet steeped in economic and technological stagnation.

Country: Afghanistan
Amount: set to receive $4 billion in foreign aid in 2017
Ruled by warlords, a country still resembling the middle-ages.

Country: Nigeria
Amount: set to receive $606 million in foreign aid in 2017
One of the most corrupt countries on the African continent, if not the entire world. Foreign aid rarely reaches the people, and merely lines the pockets of government bureaucrats.

Country: Egypt
Amount: set to receive $1.5 billion in foreign aid in 2017

Not exactly America's strongest Muslim ally. A country which has repeatedly called for the annihilation of Israel, America's strongest middle-eastern partner in the fight against terrorism. Egypt is the nation which gave birth to the Muslim Brotherhood.

Country: Indonesia
Amount: set to receive $179 million in foreign aid in 2017
The largest Muslim nation on the planet. Home to radical Islamic faction, 'Jamia Islamia'.

Country: Yemen
Amount: set to receive $55 million in foreign aid in 2017
A country which is now home to the insurgent and radical Houthi movement, which shares an incestuous relationship with ISIS and Al-Qaeda. The Yemeni populous are long-standing opponents of the west and the United States.

Country: Somalia
Amount: set to receive $196 million in foreign aid in 2017
An old stomping ground for Al-Qaeda and Osama bin Laden. A country ruled by warlords, responsible for ongoing maritime piracy. Certainly no ally of the west.

Country: Iraq
Amount: set to receive $500 million in foreign aid in 2017
A country which tore itself apart through sectarian power grabs, internal conflicts, and the rejection of democracy. Further devastated by the metastasising theocratic,

guerrilla, militaristic vacuum created under Obama's administration.

Naturally, these nations would literally starve if America refused to reach into her pocket to cover the dinner bill. Historically, the aforementioned countries have consistently ranked annually as the least performing, and the worst in economic growth. Simply put, their GDP is beyond substandard.

I'm sure anyone reading this would agree that our money is better spent back home on hospitals, veterans, education etc. Of course, the aforementioned donations do not include payments from other western countries who blindly contribute to these Muslim nations, which purport to be the evolved, "best of all peoples."

Again, I reiterate, if Islam truly is the master faith, then why does it need to survive on infidel cash? Lest we forget, the Quran proclaims that non-Muslims are nothing but filth, and will never amount to anything. In fact, according to Quran 7:179 and 6:111, unbelievers are like 'cattle' and are destined to hell for being ultimately ignorant.

> "Indeed, they who disbelieved among the People of the Scripture and the polytheists will be in the fire of Hell, abiding eternally therein. Those are the worst of creatures."
> Quran 98:6

> "For the worst of beasts in the sight of Allah are those who reject Him: They will not believe."
> Quran 8:55

If Islam lives in the west's shadow, then these proclamations only expose the fraudulence in Allah's prognostications.

Furthermore, the aforementioned donations do not include the domestic welfare Muslims predominantly rely on in the west. The benefit recipient statistics in the western Muslim community are staggering. According to the UK Equal Commissions report, it states that over 76% of Muslim women are welfare recipients, while men average around 53%.

In the United States, to curb Muslim welfare fraud, the government has resorted to the 'food stamp' scheme. However, a recent phenomenon is seeing Muslims reselling produce acquired by food stamps through local produce businesses, at exceptional profits. In 2016, a Muslim food store owner in Buffalo N.Y was indicted for misuse of food stamps by defrauding the welfare system. Bail was set at an unprecedented $2 million dollars due to the nature of the crime, which ironically is not entirely a nascent racket in the Muslim community. One would expect that these Muslims may feel ashamed about robbing the tax payer to line their pockets, yet the truth dictates otherwise. The family of the exposed Muslim criminal unapologetically voiced their distain for the west, stating "F*ck America!" But it's unequivocal that these Muslims are only emulating their prophet's dependency disorder, which I clearly exposed in my first book. The man was also a consummate pirate who possessed the inability for self-control.

Considering that the west is by far the biggest economic powerhouse in history; a civilization which has sent men to the moon, cured innumerable diseases, mastered agriculture, the arts, locomotion, aeronautics, computer technology, weather patterns - why is the Muslim nation surviving on our charity? Surely, a cursed nation as the west would yield nothing but failure. Does this mean that Allah is the god of opposites?

ISLAM'S ABYSMAL IQ RATING

According to multiple world indexes for IQ research, and the book *'IQ and the Wealth of Nations' by Lynn and Vanhanen*, the west has remained consistently around 100 IQ. The United Kingdom, Italy, Switzerland, Austria, and the United States among others have always lead the world ranking in intelligence and academic progression, not including Hong Kong, China, Korea and Singapore. If we refer to the index, it's clear that Islamic nations are struggling to keep up, never even reaching the top 10%. According to multiple IQ statistical records, Saudi Arabia, Qatar, The Emirates, Oman, Yemen, and virtually every middle-eastern nation is placed around twenty points lower than their western counterparts, weighing in at approximately 82 IQ. The same can be said for Pakistan and Afghanistan, where IQ scores are far below western standards.

Of course, the Islamic African nations were at polar opposites of the west, which is understandable since the continent has remained in a state of stagnation for as long as can be remembered. In fact, Syria and Oman are recorded to be at the bottom of the middle-eastern scale in terms of intelligence. Naturally, this could lend to the problem which has been the Syrian war; a conflict escalated by insurgents who never had the intellect or foresight to recognise that they were destroying their own country. And yet, Führer Merkel and her brownshirts insist by that allowing Syrian refugees to pour in to the EU, it makes a positive contribution in terms of academia and the job sector. The truth is that these Muslim migrants are largely unemployable, and will remain so for decades due to their cultural background.

One may think that I'm rubbing Muslims' noses in these condemning facts, but the truth is that I am unable to fathom how such an uneducated nation like Islam, who has imbibed their narcissistic prophet's poison, can even consider themselves to be "'the best of all peoples." Regardless of how much money is injected into middle-eastern educational programs, academic test scores invariably fail to rise more than the standard average. This is not conjecture, but the brutal facts.

In 2009, Jordanian Queen Rania initiated the 'One Goal' program to bring education to the Arab masses. Commendably, Queen Rania has maintained a reputation for attempting to jumpstart Arab innovation throughout her illustrious tenure as monarch. The granddaughter of a teacher, it is evident through her innumerable interviews that education itself is a priority with her directives, and a personal passion. It was the monarch who rightly stated that, "Learning to read and write changes lives, it means jobs, money, health, and dreams fulfilled." The irony is that while Queen Rania was schooled in Egypt, the monarch completed her post-graduate education in none other than Geneva, Switzerland. However, despite her efforts for a pan-Arab educational revival, the outcome has been less than stellar. In a subsequent 2013 Al-Arabiya television interview, the monarch gave a candid insight into Arab educational stagnation, which only proved that the echelon of the middle-east have been aware of Islam's shortcomings for some time.

Almost a decade later, the middle-east has torn itself apart, reverting back to religious fundamentalism, and in some regions, teetering on the edge of armageddon. It's evident that no matter how much money is thrown at the problem, the fact remains that Islam is fanatically anarchistic. There is a pervasive sense of paranoia and distrust among Arabs regarding western innovation, more so when a substantial portion of our technology is devised by Israeli companies. Adding to their paranoia comes Arab *pride*. For a westerner, or more so a Jew to outshine a Muslim, is an egregious concept for the Islamic world. No Muslim can deny that there is a lingering sense of resentment when a Muslim begrudgingly has to use infidel technology.

At the same time, the Arab community is also rigorously subjected to psychological indoctrination by Imam's who guilt the public into not embracing western ideals and education. For anyone who has witnessed Arab television through Memri TV, it is axiomatically clear that the middle-east is intellectually stunted, revelling in conspiracy theories, accusatory thought and general malaise. Some of the comments from Muslim guests are downright idiotic, some adults going as far as to use children's dolls to demonstrate how the Quran is allegedly the word of god. However, this is not surprising. If anyone reads my first book, they will know that Muhammad was perhaps the most idiotic individual in history. A man who would bathe in toilet water five times daily, dip flies into his drink, drink camel urine and believed that the sun was the size of a beachball. Furthermore, as I have already demonstrated, the man was strictly paranoid about innovation, literature, art and general progression. Thus we can see that the 1400 year old stigma has not dissipated, but is alive and well in the Arab nation today. Naturally, when 1.6 billion Muslims have an unhealthy infatuation for a paranoid schizophrenic imbecile, you can be assured that emulation is not far behind.

ISRAEL AND THE JEWS - THE MUSLIM BUGBEAR

The tension that exists between Muslim and Jew can be sourced back to the Quran, a book which openly curses Israel and calls for the murder of every last descendent of Isaac. I posit that while this is certainly the catalyst for the perpetual Muslim desire for Jewish genocide, the real source of tension is due to more contemporary issues; neither disputes over land, but the fact that Israel surpasses the Arabs in terms of intelligence, technology, security, academia, G.D.P etc.

Love her or hate her, Israel has for the longest time outshone her Arab neighbours, despite possessing little to no natural resources such as oil or gas. The country itself was built by Jewish refugees fleeing the aftermath of the Holocaust, but who possessed a fervent desire to reestablish an agricultural powerhouse. And while many will scorn Israel under the propagandist rhetoric of being an "apartheid state, who commits genocide", the fact is that the tiny democratic nation is one of the world's leading fresh citrus producers and exporters, despite the land being subjected to a perpetual drought and rocket fire. The hypocrisy of the social justice warrior is to the point of idiocy, that many liberals are unaware that their daily regiment of trendy fruit-shakes, which are no doubt consumed to cure their chronic constipation, actually contain Israeli produce. Thus none can deny that within only forty years, Israel has cultivated a long abandoned parcel of land to become respectfully known as the 'fruit bowl of the world.' For a nation which the Quran regards as 'cursed', the Jews consistently embarrass her Arab neighbours in terms of annual GDP. And just to think, Israel's economy is not based on what lies beneath, but what is harvested on the earth from back-breaking labour.

No doubt the reader has heard a plethora of anti-semitic rhetoric from the Muslim nation, where they cast aspersions, mendaciously alleging that 'the Jews stole the land' from the 'Palestinians'. However, history dictates that the Jewish refugees were granted only 10% of the land under the British mandate - 'Palestine' lost her borders after continuously failing to annihilate the Jews in joint efforts with surrounding Muslim countries. Predictably, contemporary liberal history has a nasty habit of forgetting the inconvenient and embarrassing mantras of the 'Palestinians' in the 1950's...

> "If the Jewish state becomes a fact, and this is realized by the Arab peoples, they will drive the Jews who live in their midst into the sea."
> Hassan al-Banna
> - Founder of the Muslim Brotherhood

Or perhaps we should reflect on the words of Haj Amin al-Hussein, the former Grand Mufti of Jerusalem and war criminal, who opined to Hitler that both had a common enemy - the Jews. We could debate over history, but the facts will cut through the hardest of rhetoric. The argument will always return back to historical land utilisation, as the reader needs to ask what the Arabs had accomplished in 'Palestine' for over 1000 years. History records that the region was a barren wasteland, annexed by Jordan and disregarded as nothing more than desolate. Once a Roman outpost, renamed from Judea to 'Syria Palestina' to insult the Jews after their failed uprising, never did the modern 'Palestinians' cultivate the land on the same level as the Israelis. Only when the Jews proved to be people of productivity, the rancour and resentment inevitably surfaced in the Arab people. And like I previously stated, it is the Arab pride and jealousy of those who outshine Muslims which creates the everlasting Islamic warring vacuum.

Moving away from the agricultural issue, Israel has in the last couple of decades, moved out of the agrarian stereotype to forge a bright future in technology and digital components. In truth the Jewish state has become a dominant force in IT development and engineering. Some of the most renowned inventions coming from Israel are used by the most radical of liberals *and* Muslims today. These include mobile phone components, CPUs, medical cameras, even the USB flash drive. And while the Israeli's did invent the Epilady hair removal system, I concede that no liberal woman has use for this invention - based on my casual observation of the masculine misandrists that consistently attack my work.

Only recently, Israel is fast becoming the *startup* hub of the world, where a considerable amount of independent technological advances are continuing to spring up from a nation which Allah curses. But naturally, this reflects on the ratio of Nobel prizes awarded to Jewish scientists over Muslims. There's no secret that the Jews have long dominated Nobel's long list of laureates. As the record states, there are at least 192 Jewish recipients who have been awarded in the field of chemistry, physiology, medicine, physics, literature, economics and peace. How many Nobel prizes have the Muslims collected? Twelve.

THE VOICE OF REASON

Alas, the stench of Muslim hypocrisy has hardly allowed itself to be contained. Muslims themselves are slowly waking up to the calamitous failure of their civilization, and the exponentially widening gap between the past and the future.

In 2009 on Al-Jazera news, Muslim academic and scholar Anwar Malek, besotted with the west's own prowess, candidly shamed the Islamic nation for the retrograde mess it is. His cutting words might have fallen largely on deaf ears, but the echo of reason resonates in those who can identify the problem. For anyone who has not seen this video excerpt, I can assure you that the interview was priceless. As the interviewer opened up his line of questions, the tension in the studio was palpable. As the interview began, the host maintained that "73% of our viewers believe that the Arabs constitute a great power, and have the ability to be influential." What entailed was a blunt yet acerbic response which caught the TV station off guard.

Malek retorted, "This figure indicates that the Arabs are afflicted with fantasies and obsolete bravado... False, empty bravado, which does no good to anybody. The Arabs invented, or discovered, the zero – but what did they do with it? Some of them sat on it, some put it on their heads, while others wore it around their waists, and began shaking their hips, their bellies, and their breasts, in order to sell to the world the idea that modern Arabs are doing something. Today, the Arabs constitute nothing but thousands of zeros to the left... The Arabs have lost their worth, their humanity, their culture, and everything. There is nothing to suggest that the Arabs can be relied upon to produce anything."

As the interviewer's face continued to distort, Malek unabatedly followed through with his candour...

"This false bravado is deeply rooted in the Arabs to an unimaginable degree. It is so deeply rooted that the Arabs believe they can go to the moon. If you asked your viewers whether the Arabs would be able to reach the moon by 2015, they would say: 'Yes, the Arabs will get to the moon.' By Allah, the Arabs will not go more than a few hundred kilometres from their doorsteps. These are empty words."

As the interview continued, any viewer could see the look of confusion forming on the interviewer's face. It was axiomatically clear - things were not going to plan. More so when Malek profusely insisted that, "in all honesty, the Arabs are backward, and are not fit for civilization at all." According to Malek, the Arabs have lost their identity, solely relying on exports and trivial agricultural exports to Europe. Malek continued to denigrate the Muslim nation by stating that all Arab leaders are mimetic of their predecessors, inferring that change is an alien ideology not investigated in Islam. Of course, the typical Muslim bravado was incapable of capitulating in the context, as the interviewer insisted that Islam has remained defiant to foreign occupation. As usual, Malek's response was spot on, never ceasing to inhale for a second…

"What resistance are you talking about? If you are talking about the resistance of Hizbullah – Hizbullah has destroyed Lebanon… The reality of the Arabs is one of defeat, hitting rock bottom… We are defeated, politically and militarily… and economically, socially, and even psychologically. We have a discourse of conspiracy, and we blame everything on others."

The final blow to the interviewer and the network itself came when the interviewer made the egregious error of broaching the subject of the perpetually stagnant Egypt. What made matters worse, is that the host dared to use the term 'superpower' when referring to a country which has lost three wars to Israel.

Again, Malek opened up his tirade on the small country, "(Egypt) is incapable of doing anything. It lives off American aid. Without it, they would starve. No Arab country has won a war in modern times. There has been no victory worthy of mention. All we have are defeats, which we package as victories. Look at how the Arabs live in the West. By Allah, they are a bad example. If you hear about thieves – they are always Arabs. Whenever a young man harasses a girl on the streets of London or Paris, he turns out to be an Arab. All the negative moral values are to be found in the Arab individual."

Sadly, Anwar Malek's scathing indictment of the Arab world is attributed to one individual - Muhammad and his Islam. When the Muslim scholars of days past have rigorously indoctrinated a nation for 1400 years into believing that they superior - what is there to change? Ask any Muslim in the world about the meaning of life, science, sociology, technology, and they'll predictably refer back to the Quran. *"It's all in the Quran, just read it and you'll understand"*, they'll say.

What more can be said for the Islamic nation, where the good majority still believe that the world is flat, that Muhammad split the moon, and that the sun rests under the seat of Allah? Anwar Malek's cynical yet truthful exposition of the facts, highlighted the intrinsic component of Islam - politics. Another facet which has remained obstinately incapable of progression and reform. Islam itself has not seen any diversion or progression regarding Islamic political science for over 1400 years. Muslim countries may ostensibly appear contemporarily-minded, but the laws itself are far removed from our own.

Since the time Muhammad was performing his ablutions in toilet water, what exactly has changed politically? Muslims are still cutting off apostates' heads, persecuting Jews, Christians, religious minorities and women. Gays are executed through various barbaric methods, for a crime which the west no longer recognises through common sense and reason. In fact, honour killings are now again on the rise, not only in Muslim countries, but now the west, predominantly London. Pakistan itself, the largest culprit to this particular crime, deplorably turns a blind eye to these heinous atrocities, all in the name of Islam.

In all parts of the Muslim word, it is *still* not uncommon to witness stoning for adultery, or amputation for theft. Again, I ask, what exactly has changed in Islamic politics?

The issue of women's rights in Islam, has remained unjustly stagnant. While the west sees women flourishing in all employment sectors, receiving equal pay and maternity leave, Muslim women are still forbidden from leaving their house without their husband or chaperone. In Saudi Arabia, if a woman is in need of a mammogram, she must seek the approval of her father or husband. If either refuse, her life is jeopardised. This is discounting the issue if a biopsy is necessary. However, if permission is granted, the husband or father will need to give the clinic consent to touch her, regardless if her physician is a woman. One need not be a scholar of Islam to deduce that women still have remained as second class citizens for 1400 years. Likewise, domestic abuse is neither taboo or frowned upon in Islam. Muslim Imams still condone wife-beating, and actively instruct men on television shows, while demonstrating with various implements of harm.

Of course, child rape is still a sanctified act in Islam, according to Muhammad's example, which again is causing the west to experience persistent cultural schisms due to Muslims inability to understand why intercourse with a child is abominable.

I could also elaborate in detail on Islam's regard for personal hygiene, all due to Muhammad's schizophrenic rationalisation of the world around him. If 1.6 billion Muslims believe Muhammad was the divine benchmark of perfection, then surely they too would believe that bacteria is not infectious. I could reiterate the copious amounts of Muhammad's unhygienic ordinances which I referenced throughout my first book, but I believe you get the picture. In summary, Islam is and will always remain stagnant - all due to one man, Muhammad.

The more Muslim societies fall back into Islamic fundamentalism, the more they remain retrograde and economically oppressed. And I'm not talking about the middle-east. It's unequivocally clear that Islamic influence is having an indelible and negative effect on Muslims in the west. One can witness the paradigm shift in London's east end, which has quickly become a third world sewer. Never has London experienced the apartheid driven values between the Muslim estates and its neighbours before Islamic fundamentalism took hold of the Islamic community. In truth, it was the west's influence on English Muslims which quelled their propensity to fall back into retroactivity. Today, all that has changed due to the resurgence of Islamic fundamentalism.

AN ECHO FROM THE PAST

I will finish this chapter with the words of the great Winston Churchill, who from his own observations, described a nation which is not far removed from the retrograde mess that is the middle-east today. If only our leaders bore a modicum of resemblance to the greatest leader in British history, the scourge of Islamic infiltration would cease to exist.

"How dreadful are the curses which Mohammedanism lays on its votaries! Besides the fanatical frenzy, which is as dangerous in a man as hydrophobia in a dog, there is this fearful fatalistic apathy. The effects are apparent in many countries. *Improvident habits, slovenly systems of agriculture, sluggish methods of commerce, and insecurity of property exist wherever the followers of the Prophet rule or live.* A degraded sensualism deprives this life of its grace and refinement; the next of its dignity and sanctity.

The fact that in Mohammedan law every woman must belong to some man as his absolute property, either as a child, a wife, or a concubine, must delay the final extinction of slavery until the faith of Islam has ceased to be a great power among men. Individual Moslems may show splendid qualities - but *the influence of the religion paralyses the social development of those who follow it. No stronger retrograde force exists in the world.* Far from being moribund, Mohammedanism is a militant and proselytizing faith. It has already spread throughout Central Africa, raising fearless warriors at every step; and were it not that Christianity is sheltered in the strong arms of science, the science against which it had vainly struggled, the civilisation of modern Europe might fall, as fell the civilisation of ancient Rome."

WHY ARE MORE WOMEN GOING TO HELL THAN MEN, ACCORDING TO MUHAMMAD?

It's undeniable that the radical left have perplexingly invested themselves in collective cultural suicide by promoting a religion which unequivocally advocates rancour towards women. I find it hard to believe that hardliner leftist women will unapologetically defend a faith which would ultimately have them relegated to the kitchen, and used as mere sex objects. There's an overwhelming sense of irony when liberal feminists will profusely defend a cult that advocates female genital mutilation, and the rampant abuse of women by Muslim men. These deplorable acts of barbarism are merely passed off as *cultural* issues, and nothing more. Of course, these "cultural affiliations" are deemed acceptable by liberals if they are strictly confined within Islamic *tradition*, regardless if these acts are illegal in the west. It's no state secret that Islam is not exactly the perfect addition to the left's agenda, but somehow the faith is paraded as the paragon of diversity, and a cultural necessity for broadening the west's horizons.

However, I guarantee that despite feminists jumping into the fire to protect Muslim values, and more exclusively 'equality', there is one particular tradition that not even the most ardent firebrand will be able to abide by. If only they truly knew that the very religion they laud over, not only preaches that women are inferior, but that there are allegedly more women *in hell* than men. This is not my conjecture, or a contentious argument to invoke liberal ire, but a simple fact that through *Muhammad's* inherent misogyny and gynophobia, women have a snowflake's chance in hell of going to heaven.

> "Narrated Abu Said Al-Khudri: Once Allah's Apostle went out to the Musalla (to offer the prayer) o 'Id-al-Adha or Al-Fitr prayer. Then he passed by the women and said, "O women! Give alms, as I have seen that the majority of the dwellers of Hell-fire were you (women)." They asked, "Why is it so, O Allah's Apostle ?" He replied, "You curse frequently and are ungrateful to your husbands. I have not seen anyone more deficient in intelligence and religion than you. A cautious sensible man could be led astray by some of you." The women asked, "O Allah's Apostle! What is deficient in our intelligence and religion?" He said, "Is not the evidence of two women equal to the witness of one man?" They replied in the affirmative. He said, "This is the deficiency in her intelligence. Isn't it true that a woman can neither pray nor fast during her menses?" The women replied in the affirmative. He said, "This is the deficiency in her religion."
> Sahih Bukhari 1:6:301

In my first book, 'The People vs Muhammad - Psychological Analysis', I explicitly outlined the base cause for Muhammad's inherent misogyny and his overall hatred towards women. In short, his affliction stemmed directly backed to his abandonment as a child by his mother, his self-loathing incestuous relationship with his aunt, and his over-dependence on his much older first wife - a woman 15 years his senior. These defining factors irreversibly altered the man's psyche and outlook on life, and regarding women in general. And as anyone who reads the Quran and Hadith will see, the general sense of rancour towards women is palpable.

The persistent themes of accusatory and debasing traditions regarding women's alleged deficiencies in intelligence and cleanliness, were stigmas that permeated during Muhammad's lifetime until his death. Sadly, the trend of misogyny has continued unabated for the last 1400 years. To be frank, women in Islam are literally at the bottom of the food chain. Akin to nothing more than an animal. These aren't my assertions, but the proclamations of a mentally deranged 'prophet'. In fact, it was Muhammad's 9 year old wife who stated the obvious through the eyes of an innocent and perceptive child...

> Narrated `Aisha:
> "The things which annul the prayers were mentioned before me. They said, "Prayer is annulled by a dog, a donkey and a woman (if they pass in front of the praying people)." I said, "You have made us (i.e. women) dogs. I saw the Prophet praying while I used to lie in my bed between him and the Qibla. Whenever I was in need of something, I would slip away. for I disliked to face him."
> Sahih Bukhari 1:9:490

As we can see, it was Muhammad who taught that the mere presence of a woman is enough to invalid a man's prayers. In fact, he also promulgated the concept that women are bad omens.

> Narrated Sahl bin Sad Saidi: "Allah's Apostle said "If there is any evil omen in anything, then it is in the woman, the horse and the house."
> Sahih Bukhari 4:52:111

For anyone who has read my first book, I have referenced more of these horrible accusations in their entirety. The concept behind these asinine and highly offensive teachings, is that women in general are so polluted, so inferior and cursed, that not even Allah himself can hear prayers through the enormity of a woman's stench. So much for liberals defending the alleged equality of Islam!

However, despite women in Islam facing the brunt of Islamic society's afflictions and paranoia, it cannot be denied that the ultimate insult derives not from the present, but the afterlife. As we can see from the first aforementioned verse, Muhammad went the extra mile to bolster his misogyny, by insinuating that *all* Muslim women will spend an eternity in hell. Logically speaking, how could this be?

AN INSUFFICIENT NUMBER OF PRAYERS

According to Muhammad, a Muslim must commit to a strict regiment of prayer to Allah; five times a day, for the rest of their life. What the exact number of prayers is to reach heaven was never disclosed. At one point, Allah initially prescribed 50 prayers a day before Muhammad managed to haggle with god, bringing the tally down to just 5. While the number of prayers was significantly reduced, *praying* became mandatory, and an essential prerequisite for being assessed for heavenly assignment. For the early Muslims who could not tolerate incessant bowing, kneeling, head pounding on the floor, it's apparent that many fabricated their daily tally.

However, to bandaid the situation, Muhammad once again invented a tradition by proclaiming that 'angels' kept a score of all prayers delivered. Assuredly, this bolstered a steady flow of visitors to the mosque.

> "The Prophet said, "On every Friday the angels take their stand at every gate of the mosque to write the names of the people chronologically (i.e. according to the time of their arrival for the Friday prayer) and when the Imam sits (on the pulpit) they fold up their scrolls and get ready to listen to the sermon."
> Sahih Bukari 4:54:433

So how many prayers does it take for a Muslim to *get in* to heaven? Considering that the average man would have lived around 60 years, we can deduce that from the age of 10 years old, a Muslim would need to pray a total of 91,250 prayers at the very least to be cleared for eternity; this applies to Muslim women also. The maths is quite simple:

5 prayers x 365 days x 50 years = 91,250 prayers.

If 91,250 is the magic number, and the bare minimum, then anything less is insufficient and will not grant a Muslim a V.I.P ticket to the Islamic brothel in the sky.

The problematic issue for women is that prayers are automatically invalidated upon the onset of *menstruation*. We know this is an Islamic fact, as the Hadith divulges innumerable traditions which demonstrate Muhammad literally collapsing into a nervous breakdown at the first sight of menstrual blood. Suffice to say, the 'prophet' was certainly a wuss! As menstruation can last up to five days on average, in the course of a woman's lifetime this would drastically reduce the number of prayers to an amount far beneath what is acceptable. A five day deficit in the prayer tally over the course of one's life, is an astronomical figure.

I'm sure the reader would be scratching their head over this ridiculous concept. But alas, this is the world of Islam. Nonetheless, there arises numerous questions from Muhammad's contentions. Firstly, just because a woman is bound by the laws of nature to menstruate, why should biological obligations send her to hell? Surely, if Allah was so offended by the sight of menstrual blood, and knowing that it would increase the woman's chances of eternal damnation, why did he create it? For those who have read my first book, the Hadith presents a pervasive theme of self-loathing and ostracisation when regarding menstruation. Muhammad was terrified of menstrual blood. We know this because the Hadith describes revealing stories of asinine and hysterical bathing rituals Muslims had to perform if they so much as came in contact with female blood. Again, to even touch menstrual blood would jeopardise a Muslims man's chances of entering Jannah.

Ironically, Muhammad did not entirely suffer with haemophobia, he only had issues with *women's* blood. This became a contributing factor for why I diagnosed the man with chronic gynophobia. And it is because of this negative stigma which Muhammad propagated, that has caused the entire Islamic nation for 1400 years to remain in a constant state of anxiety and paranoia - simply over menstrual blood.

STUPID PEOPLE DON'T GO TO HEAVEN?

Secondly, the issue of a woman's alleged intellectual inferiority also opens Islam up to scrutiny. Not only because it is highly insulting, but inevitably illogical. The question remains, why would Allah create women to be mentally inferior to men? Both are of the same genetic strain, but are only differentially unique concerning chromosomes. Modern science has dispelled the ridiculous notion that a woman is intellectually weaker than a man. In some cases, women supersede men's intellect in numerous fields of study. Yet Allah is adamant that a woman is somehow mentally inferior, for reasons unknown. Of course, Muslims are forbidden from questioning these teachings, and must take it on faith that the statement is true. One can imagine the centuries of women's frustrations while watching idiotic male tribal leaders attempting to solve a simple problem, all the while the women were itching to have their voice heard. Undoubtedly, Muslim women would have been scolded *"Shut your mouth! Allah says you're inferior. Let the men solve it."* And this most probably has resulted in 1400 years of societal stagnation throughout the middle-east. After all, it was Muhammad who said that a woman leader would never succeed a nation...

> Narrated Abu Bakra: During the battle of Al-Jamal, Allah benefited me with a Word (I heard from the Prophet). When the Prophet heard the news that the people of the Persia had made the daughter of Khosrau their Queen (ruler), he said, "Never will succeed such a nation as makes a woman their ruler."
> Sahih Bukhari 9:88:219

As I have already revealed, the west's IQ index far surpasses the middle-east, and in turn would mean that western women *are* mentally superior to Arab men. Surely, this fact would prove Muhammad to be a fraud.

The issue of salvation based on intelligence is a ridiculously laughable concept. To condemn a person to hell because he or she simply did not *get it*, is highly unfair on those who are born with mental disabilities or afflicted through systemic inbreeding - another side-effect of Islam, created by Muhammad. Could we surmise that Allah provides an aptitude test upon arrival at Islam's heavenly gates? Will there be multiple choice questions, or practical examination? Considering that Muhammad said that 'water cannot be defiled by anything', and that 'comets are the devil's missiles', surely even he set the bar *really* low. Even the most idiotic of women, if that was the case, would breeze through Allah's pop quiz. Regarding Muhammad's asinine contentions, it's therefore a plausible argument to say that the man himself would not qualify to enter heaven; if aptitude is a necessity to enter Jannah. How ironic it would be to see the grand master of Islam banished from heaven, while his followers walk on by with a wry smile on their faces. After all, from reading the Hadith it is clear that many of his followers had doubts about Muhammad's alleged vast intellectual capabilities. More so when the man was wading through sewerage to perform his daily ablutions...

> Narrated AbuSa'id al-Khudri: "The people asked the Messenger of Allah (peace be upon him): Can we perform ablution out of the well of Buda'ah, which is a well into which menstrual clothes, dead

dogs and stinking things were thrown? He replied:
Water is pure and is not defiled by anything."
Sahih Muslim 1:66

Nonetheless, Muhammad still taught that men specifically were destined for heaven, simply because they were predisposed with superior intellects. However, there is actually a logical argument which destroys Muhammad's assertions, of which no Muslim could deny. This being, if man was created to have superior mental faculties over women, then wouldn't his burden be far greater than a woman's? The simple fact is that any transgression he made before Allah would be *greater* than hers, for he is allegedly without ignorance, and *should've known better*. One must deduce that any creator would show grace and understanding towards his female subjects for being 'ignorant', and bearing predisposed shortcomings. Consequently, it is men who should be the majority in hell, as both the sexes are equally fallible and prone to failure in their lifetime, regardless if a woman is allegedly the lesser species. A mistake is still a mistake. We all make them. Immaterial of the minimum prayer count prescribed, men would simply not be able to keep up with prayers to atone for their transgressions. And as we can see, it's an illogical, irrational and idiotic scheme to keep Muslims chasing their own tails.

Exemplary of this, is Muhammad's teachings of the alleged Islamic end-times. For a man to proclaim that even he didn't know what the future will be, he somehow managed to conjure another ridiculous tradition which would prove that *most* Muslims are going to hell, not just women. According to the master of the universe, in the last days of mankind, there would be 73 Islamic sects established.

However, the catch is that only *one* would be permitted to enter heaven, the rest are going to hell.

> "My ummah will split into seventy-three sects, all of whom will be in Hell except one group."
> Al-Tirmidhi

This leaves the issue wide open to speculation, and equally, immense ridicule. It seems that 99% of Muslims in the future will *not* be smart enough to enter Jannah, as they won't understand the core tenets of what is allegedly the most purest and simplest religion in history. But Islam is not a simple and logical religion. It is Muhammad's *disaster-piece*, not a masterpiece. Yet the aforementioned tradition only proves that his god is an idol of irrationality; confused and incomprehensible, twisted and sadistic.

Regardless of this tradition, there still is no *logical* explanation as to why women should be singled out by Allah to face the flames. As we can see from the limited verses I have provided, nothing truly makes sense in Islam. But this is what we've come to expect from a man who invented the religion while suffering with the onset of neurosyphilis. Furthermore, there does seem to be a persistent pattern of modus operandi incorporated with Allah. None can deny that the god of irrationality has an inherently nasty habit of creating lifeforms which invariably offend him. And again, it seems that Allah revels in setting the rules in opposition. There is no balance, and no harmony in Islam. For one problem which arises, an illogical band-aid is created, to again manifest an entirely new set of conundrums. But alas, Allah is not our creator, nor does he exist, as the *logical* evidence proves.

A MAN MADE RELIGION

Islam is a man-made religion. And I mean, *man* made. The entire faith is a chauvinistic, self-serving organization created for not only Muhammad, but for men. I'm sure the reader has heard the Muslim argument that women in Islam allegedly have more rights than their western counterparts, which is a mendacious propagandist statement. This specific form of rhetoric has baffled me for the longest time, as I am still unable to fathom what *rights* they are talking about. I have scoured the entire Islamic codex, and still cannot refer to one edict which exalts women over men. There are no verses which give basic human rights to women, or prescribes that they be treated with dignity and equality. It's bad enough that a Muslim man believes he has the ordained right to rape, beat, cheat, abduct, or even murder his wife, that she also face an eternity in hell - for being a woman.

Of course, there is no Islamic hell. Hell was created on earth for women by Allah. Still, it boggles the mind why Muslim women, who are knowledgeable of these irrational teachings, still insist that Islam is the truth. The sad fact is that if any woman remains in, or converts to Islam, it proves Muhammad correct that women are intellectually inferior - but we all know that is nonsense.

It's an unchallengeable fact that women possess certain *superior* biological attributes and prowess over men in particular fields of expertise. Despite being renowned for their multitasking skills over men, they are instilled with unparalleled survival instincts, diplomacy, intuition and empathy. Likewise, the simple fact that women are inherently known to be nurturing, motherly, and compassionate, would actually place a woman further away from hell, instead of closer to it.

Stereotypically, men are known to be rambunctious, warring, short-sighted and unintuitive to emotion. If heaven is for the meek, and hell for the proud, then wouldn't there be more women in paradise than men? But alas, Islamic heaven was fabricated by a warring consummate pirate, whose unoriginal misogynistic traditions mimicked tales of Odin, Valhalla and Elysium. In ancient times, tales of heaven and celestial paradises were always allocated for warriors, the brave, the boisterous, and never the humble in heart. It's evident that *Jannah*, or Islamic heaven, is the fabrication of a rowdy, trouble-making, camel urine swilling, chauvinist dwarf with little imagination and poor taste. Surely, these logical facts only prove that Muhammad was a false prophet, and that Islam is ultimately a lie.

If we were to pragmatically evaluate both the sexes in terms of sin, how could we possibly arrive at any conclusion? Both are equal in their own respects, both deserving of salvation through humility and redemption, or destined to hell through pride. A lack of intelligence, if that was the case, does not send you to hell. Neither does your biological make-up. A benevolent, omniscient and compassionate god would understand our short-comings, and never set each sex against each other.

If logic proves Allah to be in error, then is Islam the true faith? How can Muslims reconcile the Islamic texts with the unequivocal truth?

PRIDE COMES BEFORE THE FALL

The confronting reality is that every soul on this planet in history, has had a mother. For those children who have been blessed with a loving relationship, I ponder how Muslim men would feel regarding this tradition, believing that their beloved mother would end up in hell. Or perhaps their loving wife. Surely, these irrational and cruel teachings would serve as a testing tool for the Muslim conscience - reject Islam and honour thy mother and wife, or pay homage to Muhammad and rebuke women? Like they say, pride comes before the fall.

Undoubtedly, it was through Muhammad's pride that even he was tested to the point of repugnance. In my first book, I discussed in detail perhaps the most embarrassing and disgusting event in Islamic history. As previously mentioned, there were suggestions that Muhammad struck up an incestuous relationship with his aunt. And as the fable dictates, Muhammad was distraught upon his beloved aunt's passing, to the point where the 'prophet' was driven to sexual intercourse with her corpse, to quote "lessen the pressure of the grave." Muhammad knew that his own asinine and misogynistic teachings had come back to haunt him, thus provoking him to go into damage control. You see, it was Muhammad who preached that *his* wives would be the only women in Islam to receive favour in the eyes of Allah, and to be possibly spared from the torments of hell. Thus by 'consummating' the marriage with his dead and rotting aunt, she would become one of his own *special* wives, posthumously of course.

Sadly, the karmic mechanics of Muhammad's irrational and hateful edicts certainly served to embarrass him throughout the ages, and are continuing to be a source of ridicule even today. Conclusively, the many illogical Islamic verses only prove that fraudulence is written on Muhammad's forehead, and equally on his imaginary friend's, Allah. There are no greater number of women in hell, nor is there men. No Muslim knows what the afterlife looks like, for no-one has ever returned. The same applies to hell, regardless if Muhammad believed he traveled there, despite most assuredly suffering with schizophrenia. To return back from hades is an illogical concept, concocted by an illogical fool. If Muhammad truly had visited hell, why didn't any of his followers record the stench of sulphur on his clothes, or the burn marks on their prophet's body? I'll let you fill in the gaps.

WHY IS THERE NO SALVATION IN ISLAM?

In almost every religion in history, there has always been some roadmap to salvation, no matter how esoteric the concept may be. In every major faith, there is a vague understanding of eschatological circumstance, and the prescribed guidelines to tip the balance in their favour for an eternity in paradise. Of course, this excludes Islam.

In the world of Muhammad, nothing is ever straight forward, nor does it makes sense. Islam itself is a religion covered in three meters deep of band-aids, hiding its obvious flaws and loopholes. Perhaps the largest loophole in Islamic doctrine is *salvation*. In Islam, this is an issue which ostensibly seems quite complex, yet is ultimately answered by simplicity and crushing inevitability. To be frank, there is no path to salvation in Islam. Don't believe me? Then do your own research. Gather as much information within the Quran, the Hadith, the Tafsir and the hundreds of other Islamic texts, and I can assure you that there is no *guaranteed* path to Islamic paradise. Neither is there a shred of evidence pertaining to an obscure strain of scripture which predicates Muslims' eternal salvation.

I have spent years pouring through the Islamic texts with a magnifying glass. I've listened to sermons delivered by the most venerated clerics, from both Sunni and Shia persuasion. And yet, from the years of study, the attendance of lectures, I have concluded that there is absolutely no guarantee that any Muslim is going to Janna (Islamic heaven).

For what is absolutely clear, Jahannam (Islamic hell) is frighteningly real in the mind of a Muslim. Most Muhammadans, if not all, are irremovably convinced of the existence of such a place. Muhammad spoke in great volumes of his fleeting time in the flames, more so than heaven itself. And if we were to conduct a concentrated study of the Islamic afterlife, we would see a distinct pattern of Muhammad using *hell* itself as a deterrent for people conducting activities which displeased *him*, not his god.

In Islam, hell is a frighteningly palpable concept which is also primarily used as a *weapon* to fear people into *dying* for the faith. The fear of the unknown, and the possibility of having your skin burned off and regrown daily, is a confronting vision.

> "We shall expose them to the Fire. As often as their skins are consumed. We shall exchange them for fresh skins that they may taste the torment."
> Quran 4:56

DON'T PEE ON YOUR SHOES, YOU'LL GO TO HELL

In my first book, I explained in detail from an Islamic perspective how virtually everything will land you in hell. This would include, urinating on your shoes, not praying enough, making friends with non-Muslims, owning a dog, not paying your Sharia taxes, reading poetry, appreciating art, dragging your clothes on the floor, not eating halal food, committing adultery without paying for it, not performing the hajj, not praying after visiting the toilet, leaving the toilet with the left foot, not tithing enough, touching menstrual blood, wiping your anus an even amount of times, etc. While I know the reader would burst out laughing at these asinine traditions, the sad fact is that Muslims have internalised this way of life, the Sunnah, for 1400 years. Just take a look at a group of Muslims in an Islamic neighbourhood. Notice how they all look the same? See how they run their lives like clockwork according to a religious doctrine? This hypnotic form of living is not due to religious zealotry, but out of complete fear of the afterlife.

'Doctrine' being the key word. If we were to analyse Islam solely on its merits, one would deduce that the religion is indeed primarily a political doctrine. A religion that is steeped in legislation, and nothing more. In fact, spirituality and the concept of hell in Islam is more akin to superstition. But of course, their internalisation of *superstition* is a form of emulation for their prophet's own eccentric thought pattern. But despite of this, there is one significant loophole in the Islamic system which still puzzles and frustrates Muslims even today - individual *guaranteed* salvation.

According to the Islamic texts, on the 'day of resurrection', while Allah is destroying the wicked unbeliever, Muslims are still left hanging, wondering if they themselves will face the chop. According to what scriptural traditions remain, there is certainly no way of knowing.

Undoubtedly, any Imam would white-wash this obvious loophole regarding the 'most perfect religion in history', with their own flavours and spices. A moderate Imam may state that *faith* alone in Islam and Allah will save a Muslim soul. But this would be a disingenuous statement, and an obvious form of self-wrestling; for there is no mention of *faith* in the Islamic texts that guarantees a Muslim personal salvation. However, for any true fundamental Imam, the vague promise of heaven always comes with conditions that Muslims are surreptitiously aware of, but dare not acknowledge.

The only hint that Muslims might be saved, is through 'Jihad'. And it is through this mandatory obligation which inevitably leads to radicalisation.

JIHAD

According to the Hadith, salvation can only be acquired if one is to die in the course of battle, or holy war. Muhammad explicitly instructed his men to die for the cause, under the false pretence of personal salvation. In fact, if we are to read through the hundreds of inane verses throughout books like Sahih Bukhari and Sahih Muslim, it appears that Muhammad had quickly fabricated the myth as an impromptu stop-gap.

According to legend, Muhammad's Muslim army remained in a state of apprehension when ordered to charge into battle. Yet, upon Muhammad's precipitous decree that all would dine in paradise for sacrificing their lives, his soldiers immediately marched into certain death. Muhammad never died in battle, and simply used ill-educated simpletons to sacrifice themselves for his will.

> "It has been reported on the authority of Jabir that a man said: Messenger of Allah, where shall I be if I am killed? He replied: In Paradise. The man threw away the dates he had in his hand and fought until he was killed (i. e. he did not wait until he could finish the dates)."
> Sahih Muslim 20:4678

Unfortunately, it is this Islamic tradition which explains why our world is suffering at the hands of cowardly and selfish Muslim terrorists; men who are terrified of roasting in hell for eternity. Even today, sexually-frustrated simpletons are hell-bent on pleasing their prophet by creating as much carnage as possible, for the promise of an eternity in Allah's whorehouse.

This recent phenomenon also explains why the Muslim community rarely exposes a prospective terrorist in their own community, as the tradition holds that jihadists not only pay for their salvation, but their immediate family. If you believed that the blood of infidels were the down-payment for *your* sins, would you inform on your Muslim terrorist cousin? I thought not.

> "Narrated 'Abdullah bin 'Umar: A man came to Prophet seeking permission to go for Jihad. So he said: 'Do you have parents (living)? ' He said: 'Yes.' He said: 'Then it is for them that you should perform Jihad."
> Tirmirdhi 1671

While many Muslims will downplay the word Jihad as 'struggle', the Hadith particularly demonstrates numerous traditions whereby women, the blind and the ailing, lived in a state of anxiety for not being allowed to fight in battle for their own salvation. The defining moment when Muhammad decreed that *Jihad* irremovably refers to 'holy war', was through his commandment that all who could not fight, were *obligated* to perform the hajj and pay their dues at the Ka'aba. Alas, paying one's way still gives no guarantee.

> "Narrated `Aisha: the mother of the faithful believers, I requested the Prophet permit me to participate in Jihad, but he said, "Your Jihad is the performance of Hajj."
> Sahih Bukhari 4:52:127

Or…

> "Not equal are those believers who sit (at home) and those who strive hard and fight in the Cause of Allah with their wealth and lives.' Zaid said, "Ibn-Maktum came to the Prophet while he was dictating to me that very Verse. On that Ibn Um Maktum said, "O Allah's Messenger! If I had power, I would surely take part in Jihad." He was a blind man. So Allah sent down revelation… Then the Prophet revealed "…except those who are disabled (by injury or are blind or lame etc.)"
> Sahih Bukhari 4:52:85

And…

> "It was narrated from Umm Salamah that the Messenger of Allah said: "Hajj is the Jihad of every weak person."
> Sunan Ibn Majah 4:25:2902

By these three traditions, no Muslim can deny that Jihad is defined as fighting and killing. In fact, in the book of Sahih Bukhari, the chapter 'The book of fighting' is called 'Jihad'.

MUHAMMAD IS IN HELL

However, further investigations into the texts prove that the grand master of Islam, the 'prophet' himself, made a shocking revelation which casts major doubt over the entire legitimacy of Islam. Referring to the paragon of the Islamic textual hierarchy, the Quran, it completely negates any notion of self-sacrifice. These are Muhammad's own words of doubt:

> "I am not an innovation among the Messengers, and *I know not what shall be done with me or with you.* I only follow what is revealed to me; I am only a clear warner."
> Quran 46:8-9

If there is any doubt that Muhammad was referring to his own eternal fate, I remind any critic of this claim to investigate the following tradition which was written to address the issue of Muhammad's henchman's death, Uthman. When his gullible flock inquired over the state of Uthman's soul, Muhammad retorted:

> "As to him, by Allah, death has overtaken him, and I hope the best for him. By Allah, though I am the Apostle of Allah, *yet I do not know what Allah will do to me.*"
> Sahih Bukhari 5:58:266

Surely, the most perfect religion in the universe *must have* set aside some plan to guarantee access to the throne of Allah? I'm afraid not. As I already stated in my first book, Muhammad had spent a considerable amount of time raping, murdering, stealing and in general, just living it up, that he forgot to 'reveal' the one thing that all religions are supposed to have - an exit plan. Indeed, Muhammad was quintessentially the school student who left his homework to the eleventh hour. Far too late to finish before the ominous deadline.

And as we've learned, it was through Muhammad's own bigoted gynophobia and misogyny which blind-sided him from his own hypocrisy, by dictating that all women in Islam were definitely destined to face the flames. According to him, men somehow fare better on the scales of judgment. However, there is a loophole in Muhammad's ethos, which proves obvious that he forgot the following before decreeing women would burn forever. If we are to read the Quran specifically, it's clear that Muhammad's fractured state of mind divulged a more pessimistic outlook on life and eternity; not only for women, but for the *entire* Muslim world. None can deny the following verse, which was proclaimed in Mecca, and one of the first *chronological* books of the Quran - *Maryam*.

> "It is the inevitable decree of your Lord that *every one of you* will be taken to hell."
> Quran 19:71 (Muhammad Sarwar translation)

It's evident that through the course of his career, and after all the fornication, partying, killing and raping, he forgot that he already laid the foundations that *all* Muslims were damned for eternity. Most importantly, he never considered to abrogate this verse. It's quite possible that he simply forgot.

By Muhammad's own words, every Muslim that has ever lived, *is writhing in hell* as you read this! This is not my contention, but from the mouth of the ultimate master of the universe. Pardon my frankness, but what's the point in washing one's behind five times a day, eating halal and praying incessantly, when you're destined for hell?

What's even more embarrassing, is that Muhammad claimed to be the *final* prophet, yet shot himself in the foot, as no other *prophet* is expected to augment the Quran with new revelations. What is set in stone, should never be removed. In effect, Muhammad locked the entire Muslim world in a cage, and subsequently ate the key. In truth, this irremovable verse of condemnation can never be abrogated.

I'LL PAY WITH CHRISTIAN BLOOD

Furthermore, Islam believes that Jesus was a prophet, but unapologetically rejects the crucifixion, which doubly adds to the ambiguity of salvation. Had Muhammad only recognised Jesus' ultimate act of sacrifice for mankind's sins, Muslims would have been spared. I suppose one can say it is poetic justice for a religion which is hellbent on persecuting Christians for believing in eternal hope in

Christ. Of course, through Muhammad's immense ego, and his subsumption as intercessor for all mankind, Christians ultimately have bore the brunt of his transgressions.

The issue of blood-ransoming according to the Hadith's position on atonement, has lead to a continuous environment of barbarity towards Christians, especially in Syria. During the Syrian war, a Christian nun called Sister Hatune Dogan, exposed the clandestine black-market of dealing in Christian blood. According to her, Christians were specifically targeted for sacrifice in certain slaughter factories, where the victims were drained dry. The blood was then packaged and sent to Saudi Arabia for immense profit at around $100,000 a vial, where the rich would wash themselves in blood to atone for their sins.

> "The Muslims sever the necks and collect the blood in vessels to sell the blood. The Muslims believe that if they kill a Christian and wash their hands in the blood of the Christian, they will go to heaven… it's a big business"
> Sister Hatune Dogan

It's inconceivable that this form of barbarity and unabashed paganism exists even today! But alas, this is not a work of fiction, but the confronting truth of Islamic side-effects which have been thrust upon mankind - all due to one man's shortsightedness and selfism. Ultimately, this disgusting and brutal form of blood trafficking is all in vain, considering the aforementioned Quran verse which ultimately condemns *all* Muslims.

Nonetheless, the inescapable truth that Muslims will face an eternity in hell has done little to stop jihad, and alleviate the powder-keg which has become the Islamic world. In truth, Muslims are still left holding the hot potato, looking very confused and agitated.

ANYONE WANT TO PLAY A GAME OF LIMBO?

This leads me to one final Islamic tradition dictated by Muhammad, who again offered a combined ambiguous and pessimistic revelation. In the book of Sahih Bukhari, Muhammad describes the end times in vivid detail. The ominous 'day of resurrection' would indeed be a spectacle to behold. According to Muhammad, Muslims will run around with flags on their bottoms, men will give their genitals and tongues to their 'prophet', and the Muslim Jesus will be flailing his arms like a madman, trying to kill as many Christians as possible, just after slaughtering every pig and Jew on the planet.

However, there is allegedly one obscure way to salvation, without guarantee, which is more fantasy than Islamic jurisprudence. Thus Muslims must take this tradition with a pinch of salt. Despite the Quran's authority over all Islamic texts, and negating any Islamic tradition, I feel compelled to introduce to the reader the concept of the 'Sirat bridge'. According to Muhammad, Muslims will have to cross the bridge from life to death; an instrument to gauge their faith. As the tradition holds:

> "Narrated by Abu Sa'id Al-Khudri: We, the companions of the Prophet said, "O Allah's Apostle! What is the bridge?' He said, "It is a

slippery (bridge) on which there are clamps and (Hooks like) a thorny seed that is wide at one side and narrow at the other and has thorns with bent ends. Such a thorny seed is found in Najd and is called As-Sa'dan. Some of the believers will cross the bridge as quickly as the wink of an eye, some others as quick as lightning, a strong wind, fast horses or she-camels. So some will be safe without any harm; some will be safe after receiving some scratches, and some will fall down into Hell. The last person will cross by being dragged over the bridge."
Sahih Bukhari 9:93:532

Undoubtedly, the Sirat bridge's similarities with Zoroastrianism's 'Chinvat bridge' are too conspicuous to deny. Again, it proves that Muhammad could not resist also plagiarising portions of one of the oldest religions in the world. Of course, his attempts to alleviate concerns over Muslims' afterlife were futile. Lest we forget, it was Muhammad who ultimately decided that regardless of any fantasy-based bridge escapades, Muslims are ultimately going to hell.

The inconvenient truth has left the entire Muslim nation in a state of confusion, unrest, and inevitable self-implosion - for over 1400 years. Had Muhammad truly been the most 'perfect human' as Islam claims, surely he would have had the foresight to see this iceberg approaching on the horizon. For a man who implored his people to multiply and conquer the ends of the earth, he left out one crucial caveat which would have assuredly bound the Ummah together without fail, preventing them from self-imploding.

Alas, to play devil's advocate, the man did have the good sense to create the laws of apostasy to continue his legacy. Yet, without this legislation, I'm sure Muslims would have abandoned Islam immediately after his death, upon reading Quran's pessimistic ordinances regarding the afterlife. And as history dictates, they did; albeit briefly.

However, this brings us back to the god of irrationality, Allah. Again, why would he create humans to ultimately perish in the flames? In all his wisdom, why didn't he create an iron-clad, immutable, concise and unambiguous plan to rescue his creation from hellfire? More to the point, why would you create hell, when your creation is destined to perish? The answer is quite simple. Allah does not exist. And even if he did, he would have to be the most illogical, sadistic, conniving and deceitful deity to have ever existed in the pantheon. With a fractured mind such as Allah, I'm amazed that creation exists today. I highly doubt that the incompetent god of Islam would be able to make a cup of coffee, without screwing up.

PBUH?

Finally, I feel it necessary to raise the issue of Muslims' dogmatic compulsion to continue their daily supplications with the acronym, P.B.U.H. It seems that not even Muslims can refute that their prophet is burning in hell, especially when every Muslim on the planet continues to hypnotically refer to Muhammad with P.B.U.H - "peace be upon him", the anglicized version of the Arabic S.A.W "Sallallahu allay wa Salam" (we pray for his peace).

Ask yourself, why do Muslims feel compelled to repetitively pray earnestly for the 'peace' of Muhammad, if they are adamant he is saved? This is a caveat which no Muslim has dared to inquire about, as the truth is evidently axiomatic. The hard fact is that Muhammad is *rotting* in a tomb somewhere in Arabia, and by his own contentions, is being deep-fried 'halal-style' in hell for eternity. Despite the aggrandised traditions of a man who flew on a donkey, who haggled with god, who made trees stop crying and split the moon in half, it all ends with him being worm food. Whether or not he will meet his master again, is certainly debatable and doubtful. Alas, the ubiquitous supplication P.B.U.H is the tell tale sign of insecure Muslims, wrestling with their own mortality and the ominous deadline with the grim reaper. Muslims inherently know the truth, but haven't fully realised or accepted it. Such is the power of self-delusion.

So the next time you hear a Muslim compulsively sneeze 'peace be upon him' after you say the name Muhammad, remember that they are only pleading to their god, "please let Muhammad go to heaven, because if he isn't, we don't stand a chance." The ultimate catch 22, is that by Islamic scripture it is Allah who ironically *prays* to Muhammad, not the other way around. This is a fact that I demonstrated in my first book. What *god* actually *prays* to a man, is beyond me.

> "O Allah, send *your Salat* upon Muhammad and upon the family of Muhammad, as You sent *your Salat* upon the family of Ibrahim, verily You are the Most Praiseworthy, Most Glorious. O Allah, send 'your blessings' upon Muhammad and upon the family of Muhammad, as You sent 'your blessings' upon the family of Ibrahim, verily You are Most Praiseworthy, Most Glorious."
> Tafsir Ibn Kathir - Quran 33:56

Yes, Allah prays to Muhammad...

> Ibn Abbas said: "The people of Israel said to Moses: 'Does your Lord pray?' His Lord called him (saying): O Moses, they asked thee if your Lord prays. Say (to them) '*Yes, I do pray*, and my angels (pray) upon my prophets and my messengers', and Allah then sent down on his messenger (prayer and peace be upon him): 'Allah and His angels pray ...'"
> Tafsir Ibn Kathir - Quran 33:56

So in effect, Muslims *and* Allah are praying to a dead, rotting prophet, when it should be Muhammad who prays for his people and to Allah. Welcome to the irrational and outlandish world of Islam, the brain child of a narcissistic man who got carried away with his own ego, and fell in love with his own legend.

IF SHARIA IS GOD'S LAW, WHY DOES IT FAIL EVERYONE?

Sharia law is allegedly the 'divine' god-made law which was apparently delivered by a heavy-handed angel to an illiterate, unemployed man. Ultimately, it is allegedly from an almighty god, which is purported to be the 'final solution' for all mankind.

> "This is My straight path, so follow it. Follow not other ways, lest ye be parted from His way."
> Qur'an 6:153

We've all seen the ubiquitous and ominous signs displayed at Islamic marches throughout western cities, *'Sharia is the solution for the west', 'No man-made laws, only Allah's law',* ad nauseam. However, considering that statistics have undoubtedly proven that Muslim migrants have unequivocally contributed to the rise in crime throughout the west, Muslims still fervently insist that Allah's medieval law is the absolute solution to the west's sudden increase in problems.

Not surprisingly, it is clear that Muslims disingenuously and deliberately fail to recognise that the majority of our "problems" actually stem from *Sharia* sanctioned Muslim crime against unbelievers; terrorism, rape, murder, extortion, drug-dealing, welfare-fraud, prostitution, theft, assault, pedophilia etc.

HERE COME THE MUSLIMS

Over the last few hundred years, western civilization has remained productive, excluding a couple of world wars, and has managed to maintain adequate civil stability, technological progression, and peaceful political dialogue, as opposed to the Islamic middle-east. Of course, this all changed when our corrupt western leaders insisted on more 'diversity' by opening the flood gates to Muslim immigration.

Within only a few years, crime in the west, predominantly north-west Europe, has spiralled out of control due to Muslim refugees, of which the liberal media has deliberately turned a blind eye to. It's inconceivable why these Muslims, who are allegedly escaping the horrors of war, would sully the land they have relocated to, only within weeks of their arrival.

It is through 1400 years of indoctrination into the cult that is Islam, which explains why Muslims have failed to integrate into the west. Sharia law is a criminal code which enables the wicked, all in the name of righteousness. In the eyes of a Muslim, Sharia is apparently 'beautiful, perfect and god's way.' Sadly, what Muslims cannot perceive is that through their own compulsions to commit Sharia sanctioned crimes, and to emulate their criminally-minded prophet, they not only ruin society for everyone, but equally for *themselves*. Surely, any Muslim must recognise that the west's standard of living is far superior to Islam's. We never relied on flying donkeys to land on the moon, or fabricated stories of such. We just did it. And we did so by collaborating together, with civility and reason.

If the west is axiomatically and recognisably superior to Islam's own civilization, then why do Muslims invariably fall back into Sharia, attempting to bring the west down to Islam's primitive level? The answer to this conundrum is quite simple. The idea that an infidel civilization could supersede its Islamic counterpart, is an abhorrent concept to any Muslim. Thus it compels Muslims to further dig in their heels out of pride and reverence to the Quran.

MUSLIM INFERIORITY COMPLEX

That being said, anyone can now understand why Muslim migrants are so desperate to destroy the land they have settled on - not because of jealously or envy, but due to a deep-seated reverence to their pagan god Allah; while suffering with an inferiority complex. In truth, a Muslim would rather cut off his nose to spite his face, rather than accept the truth.

For Islam to makes sense, Muslims must reverse the status quo, and bring the west to its knees, so they may ultimately provide an alternative legal system to cure the west's "problems." It's an insidious plan, which is not entirely without merit. In the bizarre and irrational world of Islam, if something does not make sense, it is automatically of the devil. Thus comes the Muslim call to rectify the problem by always introducing an unhealthy dosage of Islamic irrationality to the equation. It never works out for the best, but this hasn't stopped Islam from continuing down their path of destruction and futility.

While Muslims live in denial, they can still see that the west has surpassed all Islamic countries in terms of sociology, technology, medical science, politics etc. Constitutional republics with the incorporation of democracy, have worked splendidly in allowing western civilization to move towards the future unencumbered by despotism and religio-fanatacism. It is this glaring fact that has undoubtedly grated on Muslim migrants and their sensibilities, who have for centuries viewed the west as their greatest threat. Lest we forget, it is countries like Iran who historically coined the term "The great Satan" in regards to America and her obvious superior prowess on the world map. No doubt an irrational response, from a middle-aged culture, who are unable to fathom why such a 'heretical nation' as America prospers beyond Islam's wildest dreams.

Imagine actually being a Muslim yourself, living in a land forgotten by history, and then visiting the west for the first time. After being told since birth that "you are the best of all peoples", it would come as a shock to see all evidence to the contrary. Despite what is eternally true and irremovable, that the west has permanently left Islam in the dust, one question remains for the ardent Muslim who will die to usher in Sharia law:

Why do Muslims find Sharia law impossible to live by?

ALLAH'S PERFECT LAW?

Despite many Muslims investing their time in debauched and depraved criminal acts which are permitted in Sharia law, even they must realise that the system is too constrictive and self-destructive. It doesn't take a genius to realise that Sharia itself is inherently a self-implosive, retrograde ideology, that creates a vacuum to prevent natural progression. No Muslim can truly deny that the cause of their social stagnation and everlasting internal conflicts are due to the very laws that their irrational god had allegedly created.

The inevitable social frictions that accompany Allah's law, are unparalleled. It is Sharia's irremovable stance on inflexibility which has kept its natural progression in a necrotic state. No matter how much any hardened Muslim or liberal will attempt to sell it, Sharia law just hasn't worked out for the best. Sure, if one is a criminal at heart and has no desire to contribute positively to the world, Sharia's criminal code of conduct is apt. After all, I.S.I.S was founded on Sharia compliance and became a safe-haven for the criminally-minded. The group is, in effect, a rogue bunch of weekend warriors, sexually-frustrated losers and no-hopers, without talent or skill, who saw solace in the Islamic barbaric summer camp. Allah's law served as a platform for psychopaths to carry out the most heinous crimes in history. But lest we forget, Muhammad himself *was* a psychopath. To be fair, soldiers of the Islamic state were only emulating their psychotic prophet.

A nation built on criminality will not last. If Allah is the one true god, he should have known that the edicts he prescribed would have meant the end of the entire world. And indeed it is true, Sharia itself has indeed failed the entire Muslim world, and unavoidably turned the spotlight back on their irrational god. If the 'divine' system fails just *one* Muslim, then the construct is entirely flawed. While Muslims may try to obfuscate around the glaring facts, 99.999% does not equate to perfection. This is the inherent pitfall in labelling anything 'divine'. There's an inescapable inevitability of questioning that arises from any flawed legal system, more so if Muslims claim the legislation was penned by a perfect god.

WOE TO THE MUSLIM WOMAN

As I have already outlined, Muslim women in general face the brunt of Sharia law, without question. The alleged 'divine' law somehow has failed women for the last 1400 years. If Sharia is *perfect*, then why are women judiciously and sociologically neglected? In the outlandish world of Sharia, a woman is to receive only half of the family inheritance. Likewise, freedom of movement is prohibited without the company of a chaperone or family member. More appalling, is that a Muslim husband can divorce his wife by citing 'triple talaq', inevitably relegating her to the trash pile. Surely, any liberal blowhard would agree that these laws are far from being egalitarian. Furthermore, the law also conveniently turns a blind eye to the 'honor killing' phenomenon, as Islamic jurisprudence dictates that *apostates* must be cut off from society. However, the definition of an 'apostate' is certainly loosely applied to anyone who is deemed a threat to the insecure Islamic world - this being women in general. The stench of hypocrisy is so palpable, as it is allegedly acceptable for a Muslim man to become westernised, but never a Muslim woman. In Islam, for a Muslim woman to dress like a westerner, congruous to her new surroundings, would constitute that she is a 'whore', and more so, give the appearance of an apostate.

> "Whoever changed his Islamic religion, then kill him."
> Sahih Bukhari 9:84:57

Muslim women especially are victims of cowardly methods of punishment that come in the form of acid attacks, stoning, beheading etc, because the alleged 'divine' law fails to protect their human rights and personal safety. Alas, it was Muhammad who casted aspersions on women in general, indirectly stating that a woman was tantamount to a beast. A *thing* that any man could abuse, beat or rape. Thus domestic violence goes hand in hand with Sharia law. According to Allah, it is a divine right of men to beat their wives with impunity, free from criticism and punitive intervention.

> "As to those women on whose part you fear desertion, admonish them, and leave them alone in the sleeping-places and *beat them*"
> Quran 4:34

Not only is wife-beating sanctioned, it is strongly encouraged.

> "And take in your hand a green branch and beat her with it, and do not break your oath..."
> Quran 38:44

And then...

> "A man will not be asked as to why he beat his wife."
> Abu Dawud 2142

If Sharia is so perfect, as even Muslim women will profusely claim, then why do female victims invariably fall through the cracks? Why has the system failed them egregiously for 1400 years, and counting? Islamic legal cases in the UK have now come to light where Muslim women are pleading to Islamic authorities for protection against their abusive spouses, yet their calls of despair sadly fall on the deaf ears of the corrupt clergy. Consequently, the British police are now afraid of intervening in fear of being labelled 'racists'. If we are to play devil's advocate, how can one blame these pompous and cowardly Imams, when their mandate is to please their irrational god? According to the Hadith, it pleases Allah to see a woman viciously oppressed by man.

"Many women have gone round Muhammad's family complaining against their husbands. They are not the best among you."
Sunan Abu Dawud 11:2141

"It was the habit of ladies to support each other, so when Allah's Apostle came, 'Aisha said, "I have not seen any woman suffering as much as the believing women. Look! Her skin is greener than her clothes!"
Sahih Bukhari 7:72:715

Woe to any child who is born a female to a Muslim family. Their's will be a life of misery.

THANKS ALLAH, FOR RUINING MY LIFE

There's also the issue of criminal rehabilitation. No society is without its share of those who choose, or are forced into a life of crime to support themselves. It's an inevitable fact that western society mitigates with correctional programs in prisons. Studies have proven that effective rehabilitation after incarceration invariably sees prisoners restarting their lives by being integrated back into society with increased job-skills and contributive attitudes.

However, Sharia is completely counter-intuitive in tackling the problem of criminality. True to its irrational and fatalistic tenets, it would rather maim than rehabilitate. For the crime of theft, Sharia courts cut the hands of thieves to prevent them from ever stealing again. But from this, it creates another dilemma for the Islamic world, as the action is ultimately irreversible. Firstly, what Islam fails to recognize is that common thieves usually are from lower-social economic backgrounds, seldom without job-skills or education. Stealing is *the* only way one can survive in the unprogressive, stagnant world of Islam. If Sharia law commands that thieves' hands be amputated for simply surviving, how could they possibly support themselves in the future?

An amputee in an agrarian, impoverished society is as good as dead. Due to Islam's strict laws, the thief will become a burden on the system, as they already were. Thus in turn, Muslims will be forced to provide for the criminal they maimed, with mandatory Zakat (alms). Ultimately, nothing is accomplished. The thieves forfeit their hands for a life on welfare support. The victim gains nothing, but instead has to care for the perpetrator from their own pocket by giving alms. This is completely separate from Islamic income taxes, which is also mandatory.

Not entirely a rational and logical solution which should be attributed to any omniscient creator. Again, this cycle of violence only exposes Allah, and more so, Muhammad. Certainly, one can deduce that Sharia law bears no resemblance to any holy edict.

HOMOSEXUAL MUSLIMS DON'T EXIST?

The Islamic taboo issue of homosexuality is another dilemma for Allah's law. For anyone to give a cursory appraisal of Islamic society, it is abundantly clear that homosexuals are treated as contagious diseases, where Muslims believe it is better to kill gay men before their sexual orientation somehow magically *spreads* to the populous.

To jog the reader's memory, it was former Iranian President Mahmoud Ahmadinajad who famously stated that there were no homosexuals in Islam. An accurate statement, considering that no Muslim would dare admit to being gay in such an intolerable, homicidal and paranoid society.

> "If a man who is not married is seized committing sodomy, he will be stoned to death."
> Abu Dawud 4448

I find it timely to elaborate on this verse, which proves that there is a direct connection between the cultural stigma of Muslim men raping young boys. According to the aforementioned Hadith, sodomy is actually *permissible* in Islam if either party is *married*. This would also confirm Muhammad's homosexual tendencies, as the Quran states that Islamic heaven, a virtual whorehouse, would be populated with young boys of "perpetual freshness." It would also explain why the man was witnessed french-kissing a young boy. If the reader wishes to pursue this topic, I investigated Muhammad's homosexual pedophilia in detail throughout my first book.

Considering Islam's stance on homosexuality, it proves that Muhammad and Allah are hypocrites. As the old saying goes, it's like 'the pot calling the kettle black.' More to the point, how does other people's homosexuality negatively affect heterosexual Muslims' lives personally? Why the necessity to barbarically chop their heads off, or hang them in the streets? If the Islamic nation is compelled to conduct ritualistic witch-hunts to obsessively search for 'problems' that are clearly not evident, then something is inherently flawed in their rationality. Again, this proves that their mentality is hinged upon the god of *irrationality*.

WHO HAS THE CORRECT ANSWER?

Undoubtedly, not even the revered schools of Islamic jurisprudence could answer this conundrum, as they too are seldom able to agree on matters of legalism and reason. In fact, there are five schools of thought in Islam which apply to Sharia jurisprudence; Hanbali, Hanafi, Shafi, Jafari and Maliki. Again, this lends to the contention that if Sharia was so succinct and comprehensive, why does Islam require at least five academic faculties to interpret what should be so evidently clear? Surely, this issue must explain why the middle-east is consistently in a state of turmoil and political instability, as none can agree over matters of legislation. Of course, there's the issue of Sunni versus Shia Islam. Two societies which have never sought eye to eye on matters of legalism, regardless of the issue of succession.

It's Islam's legalistic liabilities, steeped in technical loopholes, which have paved the way for the ubiquitous Islamic clergy, despot, dictator and warlord to prey upon the ignorant masses. As I already stated in my first book, your average Muslim hardly knows the difference between a Quran and the phone book - they're just force-fed what their Imam tells them.

> "No one knows its interpretation except Allah and those well-grounded in knowledge."
> Qur'an 3:7

"Guide us in the Straight Path: The Path of those you *have blessed.*"
Qur'an 1:6-7

Indeed, Sharia law's over-bloated, technically confusing and stringent system of legalism creates a vacuum for inherent corruption from the top down. In true Islam, there is no republic, no oversight committee to monitor the echelon.

And as I previously mentioned, Muhammad himself confided that in the last days there would be 73 sects, but only one group would follow him correctly. So, from now until the end of time, not even Muslims completely know if they're following the true path. If there are five schools of thought, yet 99% of Muslims in the near future are going to hell, surely anyone would deduce that Islam fails the *entire* Ummah. Why bother to *get it right*, when the odds are against you? Muslims are surely destined to fail.

SHARIA BANKING FAILS THE WORLD ENTIRE

Of course, this two tiered despotic system is the reason why Sharia banking thrives unabated, which itself is a corrupt system that seeks totalitarian financial interest in all Muslims' business affairs. Again, the Islamic financial system fails everyone, but profits only the elite. For the layman, Sharia banking is far removed from the west's concept of finance. In the west, the banks lend a sum of money for a variable or fixed interest rate. In Islam, *usury* is strictly forbidden in Sharia law. To compensate, Sharia banks don't just lend the principle out to borrowers, they are bound by Islamic law to stake a claim in the Muslim's business, in perpetuity. Regardless if that debt is paid back, the Sharia bank will consistently retain that business' profits until it bleeds the Muslim dry. Naturally, Muslims are stuck between a rock and a hard place. They can either forfeit the business, or retain the contract allowing the bank to take financial control. In the end, no-one wins; only the echelon. And this is how Muhammad envisioned the future. It was him who would demand 15% of seized assets. In my first book, I made this abundantly clear. Muhammad dictated that 5% would go to the 'community chest' (Sharia bank), 5% would go to him, and 5% to Allah; which was virtually himself.

Ladies and gentlemen, this is a virtual form of marxism, or statism. Peasants ruled over by oligarchs. As I stated in my first book, individuality in Islam is prohibited. All must work for the state, and *depend* on the state. Innovation is leashed to the Islamic tenets, where permission must always be granted for new enterprises by Sheiks etc. Alas, they seldom are. Only if the Islamic state can profit immensely off the backs of the ambitious.

Of course, it's not surprising that the consummate pirate and Arabian mafia boss Muhammad, invented this form of financial racketeering. Islam is a criminal enterprise, devised by a criminal, who desired total control over the whole world. And this is primarily the reason why the middle-east remains stagnant, as no borrower dare venture into the devious world of Sharia banking.

LET'S BLAME THE WEST

Undeniably, there's a palpable sense of tension and unrest in the middle-east stemming from such a rigid and constrictive society, which has allowed the corrupt theocratic oligarchs to abuse their power with impunity. Naturally, open criticism of the faith, and more so the system, is punishable by death which in turn sees perennial protests lead to condemnation only of *the west*, never Islam. It is this form of disingenuous cathartic expression which grants Muslims temporary respite from their down-trodden lives, as they blame the west for all their problems and failures. However, after the protests end, the Muslims return to their homes, log on the internet, and look at their adversary with envious eyes, pondering the question 'Why can't we be like that?'

Sharia has and always will fail Muslims. Without any doubt, a constitutional democratic republic works. Especially a system based on the division of church and state. The west might have its fair share of problems, but the people have the power to *choose*, unlike Islam.

WHY IS THERE NO PROOF THAT MUHAMMAD EXISTED?

What proof does Islam have regarding the existence of their beloved prophet? The Quran? A book which was undeniably penned by multiple authors, where allegedly numerous scribes referred to a monotheistic god as 'We'? A book which possesses no chronological history, ultimately casting major doubt on Islam's authenticity and origin? Naturally, any firebrand Muslim will fight my claim on reflex, despite the overwhelming facts proving that Muhammad *never existed*.

To bolster the lie in fear that the whole rotten tapestry will unravel, Islamic 'historians' and 'archaeologists' have over time conveniently fabricated various artefacts to support their cause. Most of these embellishments are actually contained within the forbidden city of Mecca - a virtual stronghold where, for obvious reasons, unbelievers are prohibited from entering to verify said relics. Deep within the sanctuary of Muhammad's alleged tomb, contains what Islam considers the last remaining evidence of his existence - a hat, a cane, and a cloak.

Naturally, this trend of desperate fabrication has not stopped other Islamic 'historians' from conjuring more 'evidence', such as Muhammad's teeth, beard, sandals, dinnerware, or even his house. To take a tour throughout Islamic museums, it is clear that the Ummah has developed an unhealthy infatuation with a man who alleged was only a humble servant of Allah. One could say that Muslims are suffering with 'Muhammad-mania', and consider him to be nothing short of divine. Throughout the Hadith, we see a pattern of cult like adoration in the testimonies of various first Muslims. One of the most disturbing examples of this frenzied hysteria to worship Muhammad, was in the form of using his sweat as perfume.

> Narrated Thumama: Anas said, "Um Sulaim used to spread a leather sheet for the Prophet and he used to take a midday nap on that leather sheet at her home." Anas added, "When the Prophet had slept, she would take some of his sweat and hair and collect it (the sweat) in a bottle and then mix it with Suk (a kind of perfume) while he was still sleeping. "When the death of Anas bin Malik approached, he advised that some of that Suk be mixed with his Hanut (perfume for embalming the dead body), and it was mixed with his Hanut."
> Sahih Bukhari 8:74:298

Of course, there are more cringe-worthy submissions to the text where Muhammad would order his followers to lick his fingers after dinner. The list goes on.

> Narrated Ibn 'Abbas: The Prophet said, "When you eat, do not wipe your hands till you have licked it, *or had it licked by somebody else.*" i.e Muhammad's fondness for sycophants lauding over him, set the example.
> Sahih Bukhari 7:65:366

Again I reiterate, being an infidel myself, I am strictly prohibited from visiting Mecca. It is evident that whoever fabricated the legend that is 'Muhammad', were terrified of dirty kaffirs like myself pointing out Islam's shortcomings or obvious fallacies, and thus the cult remains confined behind an iron curtain.

However, I implore the reader to conduct a comprehensive internet search on the forbidden city, and witness the spectacle that is *Islamic Graceland*. Behind the walls of this mysterious city are the adornments of all things *Muhammad*. After reading numerous stories of Muslims' experiences during the Hajj pilgrimage, anyone can see that Muhammadans fervently cling to the aforementioned artefacts as the undeniable proof of their superstar prophet. However, there is just one small problem with these alleged remnants; they still don't actually prove his *contextual* or physical existence. Anyone with a modicum of intelligence can see that there is no correlation between the Hadith and the nominated effects, allegedly left behind by Muhammad. Surely, it is entirely possible for anyone to fabricate an identity with obscure belongings, such as the aforementioned. But how would anyone know if they were authentic? To substantiate the existence of an alleged individual, we must employ modern science to ascertain the truth. This is where DNA sampling is used…

NO DNA EVIDENCE

Without a certified DNA exemplar it is certainly impossible to prove the existence of any individual, even if an advocate supplied a sample of hair. For the layman, DNA sampling works by analysing a link in the biological and genetic chain. In every human cell, the transmission of genetic instructions is miraculously passed along equally to new cells, which makes DNA matching virtually flawless. There is no room for error, or doubt. However, the process *must* require an undisputed source to correlate with the exemplar. This proves to be an irremovable conundrum for Islam, as the faith is ultimately without such proof. Sure, Muslims can provide a strain of hair (beard), but who's to know that the source actually belonged to Muhammad? In all fairness, the man is a mystery, and has been cloaked in ambiguity since the creation of his identity.

Even today, there isn't one Muslim who claims to descend from Muhammad's line that has been willing to disprove the skeptics. And believe me, such people exist today. The term 'Sayyid' means 'direct descendent of Muhammad', and throughout the world, there are literally hundreds of Sayyid families all claiming to have descended from Muhammad's grandsons *Hasan* and *Husayn*. However, it would be a risky gamble for any Sayyid family member to take the challenge, as the inevitability would shatter Muslims' claims. Nonetheless, it's a guaranteed certainty that regardless of the findings, the Ummah would conspire to fix the results, bolstering the lie that is Islam.

Nonetheless, even if there *was* a perfect DNA match, which is almost an improbability, there would still be no way of verifying if the original exemplar actually was Muhammad's. The Sayyid family may just be related to some distant relative, who was equally guilty of perpetrating the lie. Likewise, who would know if the beard hair was actually genetically *human?* In reality, the 'beard' that Muslims so affectionately worship, may as well be taken from a donkey's behind. After all, it's just hair. Yet no Muslim has been bothered to substantiate the biological content of the exemplar.

Let's face it, any orphan could fabricate 'evidence' attempting to prove the existence of their biological parent. And to the uneducated layman, they would succeed. If that was the case, paternity suits in the west would skyrocket. In fact, the whole world would suddenly claim to be related to Baron Rothchild. However, immaterial of DNA sampling and its technological benefits, it is the finer details of the narrative, and the unequivocal *contextual* gaps in Islam's history which draws suspicion on Muhammad's claim.

MR. IBN ABDULLAH?

When we consider the immense contextual discrepancies in Islamic chronology, there is simply no tangible proof that Muhammad could have existed on any timeline. The argument of probability is irrelevant, and the traditions could have just been based on anyone. As I proved in my first book, the Islamic world has undeniably fallen in love with a legend, not an actual entity. For example, the name 'Muhammad' is not actually a name per se, but a generic title for a lord, a kin to 'sir' or 'his highness'. The true meaning of *Muhammad* is 'the highly praised one', a title that he bestowed on himself.

Again, this inconvenient fact of ambiguity further renders Islam's claim illegitimate. In fact, the title *Muhammad* is barely mentioned in the entire Quran. Furthermore, there is no definitive *first name* to identify the alleged prophet. In my first book, I mentioned it is possible that Muhammad was called 'Amin', deriving from his alleged mother Amina. There is also another tradition which describes him as 'an impartial arbitrator', due to this name. Considering his legacy of intolerance, petulance and inability to accept criticism, which ultimately lead to the murder of thousands, frankly I doubt this is the case.

According to Islamic tradition, Muhammad's alleged *surname* was 'Ibn Abdullah', which he inherited from his father 'Abdullah', meaning 'son of Abdullah'. But this detail is problematic, as the *name* is not definitive, but more of a declaration of faith, translated 'servant of god' or 'god's slave'. Indeed, Muhammad's alleged background is ambiguous at best. The conundrum with Arabian culture is that surnames are changed each generation when the issue inherits the father's first name. Thus it is near impossible for genealogists who attempt to trace ancient family trees in Arabia. As each generation is born, family names become so fractured that they literally can become lost in the desert. In layman's terms, there is no definitive line of patriarchal family names in Arab culture. Once you're born, your grandfather's name is negated and made redundant.

Furthermore, there is no etymological link between the surname 'Ibn Abdullah' and Muhammad's alleged clan 'the Quraysh', which apparently existed in ancient pre-Islamic Arabia. Without any archaeological records to substantiate the existence of the tribe, it is impossible to verify his name. In truth, the entire Islamic history was written *by Muslims*, not pagans. In fact, the name 'Ibn Abdullah' was bestowed on Muhammad posthumously, over 200 years after his alleged death. No historian knows what occurred before the advent of Islam. If Muhammad hypothetically did exist, we still would not be able to know his true family name. The fact that there is no archaeological and physical evidence to prove that any clan or tribe bore his family name 1500 or more years ago, is very telling, and highly condemning of Islam's claims.

Muhammad's alleged surname, or even his full name, is neither mentioned throughout the entire Quran, and is only revealed in the Islamic codex, namely by author Waqidi. Therefore, one must deduce that early Islamic historians simply made up his name, to give Muhammad some form of personification. Undeniably, his entire persona is cloaked in mystery.

THE FORGOTTEN PROPHET

Furthermore, one of the largest discrepancies in Islamic historicity is the actual time the Quran and the Hadith were allegedly written from the date Muhammad died. As secular and Muslim historians will assert, it was over 20 years after the man had passed away before the Quran was allegedly compiled in written form. The Hadith however was written by Bukhari over 230 years after Muhammad's death! Any mildly intelligent person would deduce that Islamic historicity and Muhammad's alleged existence could have been compromised within such a protracted timeframe. Why didn't the early Muslims, the foremost companions to Muhammad, *chronicle* in detail the formation of Islam in written form? Simply put, anything could have happened within 200 years. Enough time to completely omit vital details, and to fabricate stories to construct a semi-cohesive, albeit incoherent narrative. Is it plausible that for a man akin to perfection, who allegedly split the moon in half and stopped trees crying, there is not one single Muslim who *penned* these accounts? From what we know, the Hadith is entirely comprised from oral traditions, not scripture. Again, this only proves that Bukhari could have fabricated Islam from vague stories he simply *heard*, if that was the case.

Equally disturbing, is that the earliest Quran verses (revelations) were allegedly physically written on bones and wood, yet for what should be considered in the Islamic world as perhaps the holiest relics in the universe, these fragments have been ultimately and conveniently lost forever. The logical question remains, why did the early Muslims fail to preserve them in an *ark*, much like the Biblical commandment's tablets? Are Muslims stating that these allegedly holy scriptural artefacts were so important that they simply discarded them?

But if we read the Hadith, it's the Muslim trend of mendacity which has served to bind Islam together, building their feeble house on quicksand. I recall a tradition where Muhammad's 9 year old wife testified of her failure in securing a particular Quran verse on breastfeeding and stoning, whereby her sheep came and ate the sacred parchment hiding under her bed.

> It was narrated that 'Aishah said: "The Verse of stoning and of breastfeeding an adult ten times was revealed, and the paper was with me under my pillow. When the Messenger of Allah died, we were preoccupied with his death, and a tame sheep came in and ate it." (Hasan)
> Sunan Ibn Majah 3:9:1944

No Muslim can refute the fact that the Quran was most possibly fabricated by early Islamic scholars over centuries, or eaten by sheep, thus ultimately never dictated by a 'prophet'. It posits the question, how would an illiterate, ill-educated nation ever know that their 'holy' book was the product of a continuous line of fabrications? Simply put, they wouldn't.

THE MUSLIM CHAUCER

Thus far, to verify his existence, we can only rely on vague Islamic oral traditions in the form of the Hadith and the Sirat biography. However, these two venerated codexes are again ambiguous regarding *contextual* chronology and the issue of their alleged scriptural infallibility.

As Islamic history will state, the Persian scholar Bukhari allegedly collated over 600,000 testimonies and oral traditions to compile what is known as the highest authority in Islamic tradition - Sahih Bukhari. As the legend dictates, Bukhari travelled throughout the Abbasid Caliphate, recording innumerable statements from witnesses who claimed to have either known people who knew Muhammad, or had received oral tradition from their elders. And as I have already stated, all accounts were recorded over 230 years after Muhammad died.

Obviously, for a man that most assuredly never existed, the vast amount of testaments obviously did not corroborate. It is recorded that Bukhari discarded nearly all of these fictitious and fabricated stories, keeping only a fraction to develop a vaguely constructive narrative, with some semblance of convenient truth. In the end, only 6000 out of 600,000 remained. This means that only 1% of ancient Muslims were allegedly telling the truth. The rest simply made up their accounts to fill in the gaps to form a coherent narrative.

From this embarrassing historical blunder, it is evident that 10th century Muslim peasants had drunk the cool-aid, and were desperate to formulate the characterisation of an Islamic superman, no matter the cost. For what remained, there was still no benchmark to correlate the Hadith to prove Muhammad's existence. Logic dictates that just because two witnesses agree on the same statement, it doesn't necessarily equate to the truth. On the contrary, witnesses can *collude* to serve mutual interests. More so in a culture which kills apostates. One would say there is a necessity to perpetuate any lie in fear of losing one's head, if there is a possibility that the lie could be exposed.

In truth, the sheer enormity of Muslims' propensity to lie ultimately caught them redhanded. The irony is that by fabricating such inane traditions, they were damned to repeat them forever, as the

Sunnah is based entirely on Bukhari's collated stories. So, until the 'Day of Resurrection' comes, Muslims are compelled to wipe their anuses an odd number of times, pray 1825 times a year, enter the toilet with the left foot, exit with the left foot, the list goes on. All because their ancestors lied! If only they had told the truth, Muslims' lives today would be far simpler and free from the bondage of emulation to a mentally-disturbed dwarf. Ironically, as the Bible says…

"Your sin shall find you out."
Numbers 32:23

When someone is caught lying, how can they be ever trusted?

DON'T TAKE MY PICTURE!

Perhaps if early Islamic historians had painted Muhammad's portrait, the issue of his alleged existence would have been mitigated long ago. After all, every leader from every notable civilization in history has had their likeness represented on murals, tapestries, cave paintings, or sculpted from stone. Moreover, if early Muslim historians had also painted Muhammad's heirs' portraits, and their issue, we would be able to comparatively ascertain the likeness of his facial features with his kin. This alone would completely dispel critics attacks on Islam's claims. However, the Ummah is conveniently without such records, all due to one man's mental illness.

Alas, Muhammad was allegedly terrified of images. In my first book, I concluded that Muhammad's paranoid delusions derived from his obsessive compulsive disorder regarding *imagery*. But what is evidently clear, is that from a scriptural standpoint, the man rebuked artistic expression entirely as 'idolatrous'; this is the 'official' story behind Islam's prohibition of iconography. Nonetheless, this bizarre tradition which records a man literally terrified of imagery, only lends to the contention that the man surely never existed. Thus it is clear that without any iconographic proof of Muhammad's existence, the authors of Islam would need to devise a tangible reason for the lack of artistic evidence. By concocting a far-fetched story of a paranoid dwarf who suffered with the worst form of neurosis, it gave some scientific credibility to Islamic history to explain Muhammad's absence from the artistic world. It's abundantly clear that whoever fabricated the Muhammad identity, they needed to create such an outlandish story that even the most skeptical Muslim would not dare probe the issue.

What is certainly vexing and highly revealing for the Islamic world, is that there are no ordinances in the Quran that actually forbids *paintings* of people. Only idolatrous graven images of 'deities' are forbidden. Since Muhammad vehemently preached that no man can be called god, this would exclude himself. There are multiple verses throughout the text which confirm this, namely Sura 31:13, 4:48, 4:116, 39:65 among many others. Yet none of these verses mention 'imagery' or 'pictures'.

If we trace back to the first Islamic texts, what we can deduce is that the Quran was created to mimic Judaism, borrowing heavily from Jewish tradition, and equally minor themes from the New Testament. The Quran's first authors loosely pieced the Islamic narrative together on various parchments, while flippantly basing the incoherent story on a fictitious prophet. The Quran itself is not a chronological story, but merely hints of Biblically plagiarised events, made to fit with Muhammadan Islam. It's most probable that the Arabs circa 750 A.D onwards, required a new religion for themselves to band an empire together. After all, historians have noted that during the first Arab conquest of Jerusalem, the 'barbarians' presented no religion resembling Islam, nor bore the symbol of any god, let alone Allah or his prophet.

The capture of Jerusalem by the Arabs in late 630 A.D was not a bloody takeover, but achieved through peaceful negotiations - wholly contradictory to the Quran's murderous edicts. The Channel 4 documentary 'Islam - the untold story' headed up the investigation, revealing condemning facts to trump Islam's alleged history.

> "The truth of the matter is we don't know what was the true religion of the first Arab conquerers."

Historically, the first Arab conquerer to take Jerusalem was called Muawiyah, a warlord. But as the documentary states, if the leader was a Muslim, he showed very little sign of it.

> "The astonishing thing is that nowhere, not on his inscriptions, not on his coins, not on any of his documents, is there so much as a single mention of Muhammad."

Thus is the mystery that is Islam.

200 years after the Quran was compiled, it is clear that the rabble became increasingly dissatisfied with Islam's gaping loopholes in its historicity, and cried out for clarification. It is understandable why Bukhari was commissioned to create a whole catalogue of Islamic history, including *Muhammad* himself. As it would be too late, and far

too conspicuous for any painting of 'the prophet' to suddenly appear after said inquiry, Bukhari went in to damage control, fabricating Muhammad's eccentric fear of imagery to explain the absence of such evidence. This somewhat plausible argument would serve to quell Muslims' curiosity, but at the same time, leave the faith open to criticism for centuries to come.

THE MAN WHO WASN'T THERE

According to legend and contemporary scholars, Bukhari actually travelled *alone* to the farthest reaches of the caliphate. We know this because the man never made mention of any companions during his journey. Furthermore, there were no witnesses to his travels. No archives or census records, no account of toll and taxation, nor official written prose by clerics to commemorate such an honourable guest. One must agree with the possibility that Bukhari simply made up his stories, fabricating vast accounts from witnesses that also probably never existed. After all, Bukhari was a highly proficient and intelligent scholar. It's quite possible that he could have applied his intellect to manufacture the legend of Muhammad, basing him on various historical individuals, tribal leaders etc.

Returning empty handed to Baghdad (the capital) would have cast a shadow on his career, and undoubtedly put his life in jeopardy. Failure was not an option. To inform the high command that all accounts were fictitious, uncorroborated and vague, would have infuriated the zealous echelon. If word of Muhammad's non-existence had reached the masses, the entire Islamic establishment would have come crashing down. The Islamic caliphates had worked hard to suppress the people, and Bukhari's mandated work would have served their interests by inventing the Sunnah, which is based on the Hadith, to further oppress Muslims.

As I have already explained, the Sunnah is a rigid set of legalistic ordinances that Muslims are commanded to follow. Perhaps it is for this reason why Bukhari was commissioned - to bolster the lie to further their corruption, entangling the common Muslim in a web of ordinances and supplication. Naturally, this conjecture is not without merit, as one needs to ask themselves how Muslims practiced the Sunnah *before* the Sahih Bukhari codex was published. Conclusively, the aforementioned facts only prove that Islam has amounted to one lie being built on top of another.

WHY IS THERE NO PROOF THAT ISLAM EXISTED BEFORE MUHAMMAD'S BIRTH?

While many will attribute the creation of Islam to Muhammad, the actual history of the faith contradicts this widely spread belief. In truth, and according to the Islamic scriptures, the religion has always been in existence before the creation of mankind. As Muhammad arrogantly claimed, Islam precedes all cultures, creeds and religions, exalting itself as the paragon in the pantheon. The Quran itself is the alleged testament of one man being chosen to re-reveal the true word to the world, correcting the wicked Jews and their perversion of the master faith.

Although, Islam's assertion is beyond the realm of far-fetched superstition; it's absurdity defined. According to Muhammad, it was Adam (the first human) who was actually *a Muslim*. Allegedly also, Abraham was a Muslim, Noah was a Muslim, Moses was a Muslim - even Jesus of Nazareth was a Muslim. Islam teaches that not only were every Biblical character in history was a Muslim, but even *you* were born a Muslim! I kid you not.

Referring to the Quran, it is your parents who pervert your true faith, imposing their own religion on you.

> "And when your Lord took from the children of Adam - from their loins - their descendants and made them testify of themselves, [saying to them], "Am I not your Lord?" They said, "Yes, we have testified." [This] - lest you should say on the day of Resurrection, "Indeed, we were of this unaware."

Quran 7:172

"No babe is born but upon Fitra. It is his parents who make him a Jew or a Christian or a Polytheist."
Sahih Muslim 33:6426

NO CONVERTS, ONLY REVERTS

Indeed, the mythical character 'Muhammad' was so obsessed with the concept of 'religion', he believed that all mankind was genetically fused with Islam. A mendacious insinuation that all men are umbilically attached to the faith, and thus inherently know the truth. Hence, whenever a person converts to Islam, they are surreptitiously referred to as 'reverts' by the Muslim community, but publicly paraded as 'converts'. Yes, you heard correctly. Converts are actually reverts. Still following? I'll continue. Not even the greater majority of new Muslims are aware of this asinine and presumptuous ideological paradox, as those who embrace the faith indeed invariably refer to themselves as 'converts'. Did Cat Stevens purport he reverted to Islam? Or did Mike Tyson himself publicly state that he was reverting back to the true faith? Of course not. Simply because it doesn't even make sense to new prospectives. In fact, many Muslims themselves don't truly understand the concept. Simply because the logic is so outlandish, that to give the notion a moments thought would invoke a migraine.

Alas, this presumptuous method of thinking is the predictable hallmark of Muhammad; a man addled with chronic insecurity, it would provoke him to fabricate such a ridiculous notion. Naturally,

Muhammad's absurd theory is a convenient stopgap for a man who was inexplicably a die-hard pagan for over 40 years, despite claiming to be god's perfect messenger. Indeed, it was the *only* explanation for such a deplorable lifestyle.

How could Allah choose such a depraved man to lead a 'righteous' nation, a man who danced around the Ka'aba naked, and embroiled himself in ritualistic orgies, among other cultural affiliations? Surely, even Muhammad himself realised his vulnerability to criticism, especially when the alleged 'master of the universe' was born into an idol worshipping, fertility cult. Being a pathological narcissist, his asinine and far-fetched theory of 'reversion' would paper over his glaring hypocrisy, and inevitably silence critics of the faith.

CONVENIENT DISAPPEARANCE OF THE ANCIENT ISLAMIC WORLD

Furthermore, as Islamic legend dictates, up until some point in history, the entire world was actually Islamic. Allegedly, ancient civilisations on all continents were built on the fundamentals of Islam. This would mean that these communities employed Sharia law, where women dressed in Burqas, everyone had a copy of the Quran, and all men flew around on flying donkeys. Allegedly, Islamic architecture and mosques dominated the landscape, and all citizens spoke Arabic. After all, according to Muhammad, only Allah can speak Arabic. I refer to this with Quran 12:2, 42:7 and 41:44.

Likewise, Adam himself was allegedly 27 meters tall, which would mean that mankind was significantly taller than today's standards; thus easily traceable.

So, how did it all go so wrong? Why is 3/4 of the world today non-Muslim? Where are the mosques of old? Where are the original

Qurans predicting the coming of a super-prophet? And more importantly, what happened to the flying donkeys?

As I have already stated, according to Islamic sources, the origin of the world's problems predictably stem all the way back to 'the Jews'. Muhammad believed that the tribe of Israel had corrupted the word of Allah by conspiring to fabricate the Torah - an alleged heretical document, mandated to erase Islam forever. Ask any Muslim today, and that is the standard answer they will give you.

> Narrated Ubaidullah: Ibn 'Abbas said, "Why do you ask the people of the scripture about anything while your Book (Quran) which has been revealed to Allah's Apostle is newer and the latest? *You read it pure, undistorted and unchanged, and Allah has told you that the people of the scripture (Jews and Christians) changed their scripture and distorted it, and wrote the scripture with their own hands and said, 'It is from Allah,' to sell it for a little gain.* Does not the knowledge which has come to you prevent you from asking them about anything? No, by Allah, we have never seen any man from them asking you regarding what has been revealed to you!"
> Sahih Bukhari 9:92:461

Thus, the Torah's own existence would inevitably validate Muhammad's prophethood and his own self-proclaimed mandate to cleanse the world of 'Zionism'.

"I will expel the Jews and Christians from the Arabian Peninsula and will not leave any but Muslims"
Sahih Muslim 4366

Abu Huraira reported Allah's Messenger (may peace be upon him) as saying: "The last hour would not come unless the Muslims will fight against the Jews and the Muslims would kill them until the Jews would hide themselves behind a stone or a tree and a stone or a tree would say: Muslim, or the servant of Allah, there is a Jew behind me; come and kill him; but the tree Gharqad would not say, for it is the tree of the Jews."
Sahih Muslim 41:6985

Thus the reader can understand why the entire Islamic world is hell-bent on wiping Israel and the Jews off the face of the planet. Of course, this is cultism defined. All cults nominate a foe, internalising persecution, paranoia, and vehemently persist in the annihilation of their enemy to honour their leader. Ironically, Muhammad failed to understand that being Jewish was not only confined to faith, but also genetics. He had no idea that Jews were a *race* of people. A glaring biological fact that even the grand master of the universe could not comprehend. Thus, the man insisted that 'the Jew', was just a religion, and a perverted form of a Muslim. Nothing more.

THE NIGHT JOURNEY

The keystone Islamic tradition, 'the night journey', signifies Muhammad's ascension to the heavens to receive his coronation above the prophets, and fealty from Allah. Yes, you heard correctly. The Islamic texts state that Allah swears allegiance to *his* prophet, and prays to *him*. Don't believe me? Here is the verse in all its glory...

> Ibn Abbas said: "The people of Israel said to Moses: 'Does your Lord pray?' His Lord called him (saying): O Moses, they asked thee if your Lord prays. Say (to them) *'Yes, I do pray*, and my angels (pray) upon my prophets and my messengers', and Allah then sent down on his messenger (prayer and peace be upon him): 'Allah and His angels pray ...'"
> Tafsir Ibn Kathir - Quran 33:56

As we can see, Allah was nothing more than a sock puppet for Muhammad, and unquestionably bent his will to his creation. As I have stated in my first book, it is evident that Muhammad therefore exalted himself as god, while suffering with a messiah-god complex. It wasn't Allah who created Muhammad, but vice-versa.

The Quran's account of the 'farthest mosque' unquestionably proves that Islam teaches that the faith was originally established before all subsequent religions. In regards to the 'night journey, there is one small problem with Muhammad's tall tales of his flying donkey escapades to the alleged 'the farthest mosque'; he failed to divulge the actual *geographical* region of this highly significant location. Conveniently, only when the Hadith was written 230 years after his death, the city of 'Jerusalem' was nominated as the location of the mosque, Today, the 'temple mount' is alleged to be the actual point of his ascension, which explains the ongoing conflict between both Jewish and Muslim communities in the ancient city. From a historical standpoint, Jerusalem has always been a city for the Jews, which was built by Jews, for the Jews, for a Jewish God. Muslims are simply occupying the land out of ignorance, due to the Hadith and Bukhari's mendacious fables.

And while the entire Muslim world would call for my death for speaking this simple truth, what Muslims cannot refute is that 'Jerusalem' is never mentioned in the entire Quran! Neither is the name 'Palestine' written throughout the 114 chapters. The fact is that Muhammad was a liar, and never in his lifetime visited Israel. Indeed, the parallels between Islam and Shakespeare are staggering. For the layman, there has been for some time great contention in the academic world, where ardent advocates are now doubting the authenticity of Shakespeare's work. For a man who was neither gentry, nor travelled to exotic locales, it casts doubts on the playwright's ability to imagine such imaginative and timeless poetry. Thus, historians are now deducing that the works are to be attributed to a royal contributor with formal education, and traveling experience, much like Bukhari.

How could Muhammad possibly know what Jerusalem looked like? Why would Muhammad state that there was a grand mosque in the city, when there has never been any recorded landmark? It seems that the author of Islam, Bukhari, forged an entire anthology of fables to substantiate fiction as fact. Conveniently, it is obvious that the early Islamic scribes of the Abbasid empire nominated the city of Jerusalem, especially after the caliphate's conquest of Syria-Palestina (Judea).

Again, it's profoundly undeniable that Bukhari and early historians filled in the gaps to the Quran's vague historical accounts. Suspiciously, the night journey itself isn't even written on the Dome of the rock or the Al-Aqsa mosque in Jerusalem, the alleged location of the ascension! This is highly condemning of Islam. No Muslim can ever explain this gaffe.

Despite the remains of a grand Israelite temple existing today in Jerusalem, the problem with Islam's claim is that there is a distinct lack of evidence to prove that the edifice itself was ever a mosque. Even today, no Muslim has ever uncovered tangible archaeological proof to verify Muhammad's claim. Of course, any Muslim would insinuate that it was the Jews who are guilty of erasing history. But history can never be erased, as archaeology is self-revealing. Thus there are no hidden Islamic inscriptions, nor does the temple mount itself conform to Muhammad's physical description of the mosque he traveled to. Simply put, the authors made it all up. As I mentioned in my first book, it is obvious that the character 'Muhammad' was based on a number of individuals. One of them most likely suffered with schizophrenia, which would explain the fantastical tales of a 'prophet' *imagining* that he flew to Jerusalem on a flying donkey, before ascending to heaven.

NO RECORD OF ISLAM OUTSIDE OF ARABIA

What we can ascertain, is that without a shred of evidence, there is absolutely no proof that *Islam* ever existed before Muhammad was born. For a religion that was ordained by an almighty god himself, it boggles the mind how he would allow Islam to be wiped clean from history. The Bible itself has stood the test of time, despite many attempting to destroy and pervert it. All attempts have failed. Yet, Islam, the religion that exalts itself over all, comes up short with any explanation for mankind's prowess over Allah.

Surely, another logical argument would prove that not all of mankind were allegedly wicked enough to reject Allah's word before the advent of Muhammad. There must have been some who were dedicated to the faith, inscribing their account and the 'truth' on parchments, cave walls, coins, art, weapons etc. Yet there is simply no evidence. The history of the world as we know it predates modern civilisation as far back as 10,000 years. According to Muhammad, the stone age would have indeed complied with Sharia law. Yet, from the innumerable cave paintings that have been discovered, there is no traceable evidence of Islamic influence. While any Muslim will argue that Islam was centralised in Asia Minor, this would conflict with Muhammad's contentions. According to him, the *entire* world was *Muslim* at one point in history. We know this due to the 'reversion paradox', among other traditions within the Islamic codex.

If that was the case, then why is there insufficient evidence to prove his claim? No hard-line Muslim can escape the inevitable truth that all ancient cultures throughout the world bear no resemblance to Islam.

The ancient Australian aborigines predate Muhammad by nearly a thousand years. Decorated inside the caves of the Arnhem land region, are paintings venerating the 'rainbow serpent' and other pagan fertility affiliations. Still, there is no depiction of Islam among their artistry. Likewise, the ancient Egyptians precede Islam by over 4000 years, yet there are no recorded accounts of any mosque, Islamic prophet, or any law resembling Sharia. From we have learned, the Egyptians were strictly polytheistic, and deified the pharaohs. This teaching in itself is abhorrent to Islam, as the Quran states that the *monotheistic* 'Allah' bears no children.

Even the ancient south-american civilisations predate our own by at least 4000 years, more specifically the Mayan peoples, which can be traced back as far as 2000 B.C. All of these cultures were steeped in rich mythology and paganism, yet are far removed from Islamic theology and practices. Much like the ancient Egyptians, the south Americans invested in idol worship, and charting 'solar' cycles, namely eclipses. This was done to placate and manipulate the masses. However, Islam is a religion based on 'lunar' cycles. It is inexplicable why these cultures suddenly shifted away from the ordained 'moon' worship, to conventional solar cycles. The only explanation is that Islam never existed during these ancient eras.

WHERE'S ADAM'S REMAINS?

As I have previously stated, the Hadith divulges the actual height of Adam; this being a ridiculous 27 meters tall (60 cubits).

> The Prophet said, "Allah created Adam, making him 60 cubits tall."
> Sahih Bukhari 4:55:543

Not exactly an unmissable human in terms of stature. And yet, there is no reason given for this inexplicable and implausible embellishment. It is what it is. Just another fabrication, a 'tall' tale, deriving from the fractured mind of Bukhari.

Considering the genetic ramifications of being endowed with such vertical prowess, it is fair to say that Adam's own offspring would equally be as tall as him. And as Islam will have it, Muslims have allegedly walked the planet for millennia, allegedly reproducing in the likeness of their patriarch. If that was the case, surely there would be literally millions of skeletal remains around the world, albeit fossilised, found within only a shallow depth of the earth. After all, Islamic traditional rites state that Muslims *must* be buried only enough to cover the body. Thus logic would dictate that anyone living in the middle-east would be able to easily uncover Adam's descendants' remains which undoubtedly would bear the likeness of such mystical humans.

Not surprisingly even today, despite archaeologists continuing to uncover bizarre remains of early hominids, *none* have uncovered so much as a bone which correlates with the Islamic Adam, and his kin. If the Muslim world did however discover such evidence, I can guarantee that we would never hear the end of it. Indeed, Muslims are predisposed to hysterically holding up any 'evidence' which they claim substantiates the Quran, whether it be a tooth, or hair from a donkey's behind. But apart from this, the logic behind 27 meter tall humans is quite baffling. Simply put, the human race is actually increasing in stature, not shrinking as Islam claims.

Over the last millennia, the world has witnessed humans persistently growing far beyond their ancestors' physical height. In fact, within only the last few hundred years, mankind has increased its average height by almost 10 cm. According to scientific research, the human race has increased its statute by at least 40 cm since the time of Christ. During the 1st century, the average man was estimated to stand around 5ft 1in. Today, men are measured at approximately 5ft 9in.

Alas, the fables of Adam and Muslim giants are another embarrassing tradition which only proves that the Islamic scriptures are replete with mendacity.

THE SCAPEGOAT

Again, in accordance with Muhammad's claim, it was 'the Jews' who perverted the word of Allah. How could this be possible if the entire world outside Asia Minor has no record of Islam existing 2000 years before Christ's birth? What would be there to 'pervert'? Furthermore, the Jews never ventured further than Egypt and Canaan before Muhammad's birth, and were told by the God of the Bible to dwell only in *Israel*. History dictates that the diaspora occurred during 77 A.D. If the Jews were officially recorded to have been expelled from the homeland 4000 years after the south American peoples existed, how could they have erased Islam from those regions? Muhammad's assertions simply do not make sense.

Logically speaking, regardless of alleged Jewish conspiracies, it's also unfeasible that the entire world would conspire in a coordinated conspiracy to erase Islam from history. For what reason would they do this? Surely, such a feat would be impossible without a global communication network. Thus there is simply no motivation for them to erase their own culture. If Islam is allegedly perfect, and the solution for mankind, why would they destroy their harmonious utopia, or allow the Jews to do so?

Of course, it was Muhammad's wild imagination and paranoid delusions of this alleged chain of events which he believed would validate his homicidal mandate to kill all unbelievers, especially Jews. After all, anyone who denies Islam would be complicit in the conspiracy. Such are the hallmarks of a paranoid schizophrenic. The mere act of perceived insubordination, in the mind of a twisted, disturbed individual can lead to disastrous results.

What Muhammad could never comprehend, is that in every ancient civilisation, there has always been a detailed *written* account of their culture, history, patriarchy, monarchy, and religion, which are invariably inscribed on their walls or on papyrus. I have conducted a thorough analysis and study of virtually every known culture that existed over the last 10,000 years - none bear any similarities to Islam. In fact, as my first book detailed, it was actually Islam which evidently plagiarised portions from its surrounding cultures, but conveniently never from ancient civilisations across the Pacific, Atlantic and Indian oceans. While Muslims today will accuse virtually any culture of erasing Islam, the truth is that the most fervent abrogators of history have failed. I make mention of the ancient Egyptian Queen Hapshetsut in my first book. I find it fitting to reintroduce the history of this fascinating monarch, whom defied the misogynistic patriarchy. Despite their efforts to erase her from history, her legend remained unsuppressed as the truth of her majesty revealed itself over centuries. Case in point, you can't erase all history.

For whoever wrote the Hadith, it is clear that early Muslims' lack of imagination motivated scholars to borrow heavily from foreign cultural themes and directly from Hindu-Buddhist folklore, Zoroastrianism etc. Ironically, none of these cultures bear the slightest historical account regarding derivative works stemming back to the alleged Islamic era before Muhammad's birth. There is no written evidence, no inscriptions, or artefacts. And more importantly, in the last 1400 years, there has been no record of rediscovered Islamic history predating Muhammad, using the best archaeological technology known to man.

The irony is that Muhammad's distorted and confused retelling of history relies heavily on the religion he hated, Judaism. According to

Islamic sources, the Ka'aba was allegedly built by Abraham and his son, Ishmael. For what reason the father of Judaism would travel as far as Saudi Arabia to build a *box*, is unknown. However, contemporary historians have discovered that the origin of the banal-looking house of worship actually derived from Yemen, and could not have been built by the aforementioned Biblical characters. Thus the issue of historical veracity continues to plague the Muslim world.

THE PALESTINIAN MYTH

Conclusively, the entire Muslim world have bought into the fallacy that their religion existed since the dawn of time. It's evident that *lying* has played a considerable role in solidifying Islam, allowing it to fester and spread into contemporary times. One can say that this trend of embellishment also contributes to the ongoing myth that Palestine was once a sovereign nation, of which the polarising issue has caused immense contention worldwide.

If we were to investigate the Palestinian claim, again we see that the facts simply do not add up. It's crucial to broach this subject, as the Muslim hierarchy has deluded modern-day Arabs into believing that the land of Israel itself was always Islamic. However, the absence of proof is staggering, and surely condemning. Simply put, if 'Palestine' is a lie, it invalidates the nation's barbarity towards the Jews, and their hostile approach to regaining land that they never truly had a right to claim. Again I reiterate, 'Palestine' is never mentioned in the Quran.

The deceased Yasser Arafat, actually a native Egyptian, still bears all culpability for fuelling the Palestinian agenda. It was Arafat who claimed that the fictitious country had existed for thousands of years, which is a total fabrication, and a perversion of the truth. One needs only to think upon the aforementioned Islamic history to understand where the man acquired his taste of mendacity. Ironically, had Arafat only supplied a shred of evidence to prove that an *ancient* Palestine once retained sovereign laws, an economy, currency, culture, a unique flag, or a national anthem, then the issue would have been mitigated.

Can any Muslim today name one ancient Palestinian king? Who were his issue or consorts? Their answers will always come up short. Indeed the former monarch of Jordan, King Abdullah in 1948 once dispelled the myth by stating that "Palestine and Jordan are one." This would explain why the 'Palestinian' and the Jordanian flag today are almost identical. The truth is that 'Palestine' was once known as cis-Jordan, or trans-Jordan, and were ruled under the British and Jordanian Mandate.

The actual name 'Palestine' is somewhat of a misnomer. The fact is that Judea was subsequently renamed 'Syria-Palestina' by the Romans to undermine Israel's sovereignty as a form of punishment, after their failed revolt. The original *Philistines*, or Palestina, were not actually Arabs. They are historically regarded as peoples from the Aegean, otherwise known as 'The Sea Peoples'. Only recently, archaeologists in Israel have uncovered large quantities of Philistine artefacts, which have given a detailed account of their former life in the land. It seems that the Islamic claim to the land is again moot, as the relics found bear no resemblance of Islamic art, nor make mention of Allah.

These inconvenient facts still have not stopped Islam from fuelling the agenda to invoke sympathy for Palestine, and to use the people as sacrificial lambs for their cause. In truth, the oil-rich Arab states could have alleviated Palestine from her woes, but they keep her on show like window dressing to undermine her Jewish neighbours. For a Muslim, it's better to live the lie, than face the truth. And thus summarises Islam as a whole. A religion that was built on lies, which encourages mendacity, to cover up its never-ending falsehoods. Evidently, Islamic history fails to corroborate with natural history. The Islamic narrative is so full of holes, the entire story cannot hold water.

HALLMARKS OF A CULT

Unquestionably, Islam is another product of a false prophet's imagination. Lying to substantiate a bogus claim is a concept far from nascency. Without the body of evidence, those with ulterior motives must cross the threshold into fiction to achieve their goals. Joseph Smith, founder of the Latter Day Saints, is equally guilty of fabricating lies to edify his claim. According to Smith's erroneous contentions, native Americans were apparently the lost tribe of Israel. However, DNA sampling quickly put an end to that theory. Naturally, Smith never had the foresight to realise that future technology might one day trump his claims. Thus is the power of self-delusion and one man's ambition to fool the world.

If there is no prerequisite to prove the existence of an ancient religion, anyone could claim that they were sent by a god to rectify history. Of course, it would only make sense for the creators of Muhammad to fabricate the myth of ever-existing Islam. Surely, if the religion was ostensibly nascent, many would question why Allah waited thousands of years to reveal the 'truth'? This loophole would indeed cast immense doubt on Muhammad. Empirical evidence would only prove that Islam was merely an afterthought of a growing Arab civilization seeking to forge its place in the annals of history.

Unfortunately for Islam, it must rely solely on Muhammad's word alone - a man who clearly did not exist. It seems that the art of *the lie* is the glue which binds Islam together, and will always continue to be, in aiding in its agenda. But the strongest of adhesives always dissolve under extreme heat. The *heat* that is immense scrutiny and logic.

History has an inherent, and sometimes inconvenient way of revealing itself, no matter how deep it's buried. As previously mentioned, Muhammad is certainly a mystery. Thus I find it fitting to quote the Bible, a book which warns of an end times religion, the embodiment of a mysterious individual who will deceive the entire world.

> "And upon her forehead was a name written, *Mystery*, Babylon The Great, The Mother Of Harlots And Abominations Of The Earth. And I saw the woman *drunken with the blood of the saints, and with the blood of the martyrs of Jesus…*"
> Revelation 17:5-6

And…

> "He will go out to *deceive the nations* - in every corner of the earth. He will gather them together for battle - a mighty army, as numberless as sand along the seashore."
> Revelation 20:8

WHY IS ISLAM NEVER MENTIONED IN THE BIBLE?

It is important to clarify Muhammad's position on the Torah and the New Testament before stating the obvious. As the reader will quickly learn, there is absolutely no mention of Islam throughout the entire Bible. This is problematic for Islam as it was Muhammad himself who believed, in all foolishness and evidently short-sightedness, that the *original* Bible was allegedly proof that Islam is the true faith. As the Islamic texts describe, the 'prophet' actually *swore* upon the Torah (Tanakh) and Christian texts in a poor and foolish attempt to validate his prophethood. According to Islamic scripture, Allah gave an Islamic Torah to Moses, and the Injeel (New Testament) to the people of the book (Christians).

As we can see, the illiterate father of Islam wholeheartedly believed through self-delusion that the original Mosaic law was completely compatible with Sharia law.

> "They said: Abul Qasim, one of our men has committed fornication with a woman; so pronounce judgment upon them. They placed a cushion for the Apostle of Allah, who sat on it and said: Bring the Torah. It was then brought. He then withdrew the cushion from beneath him and placed the Torah on it saying: I believed in thee and in Him Who revealed thee." Sunan Abu Dawud 38:4434

What is most condemning of Muhammad's claim to prophethood, is that the actual Torah's eschatological narrative and Mosaic law are far removed from Islam's, albeit for a few legislative edicts that

Muhammad obviously borrowed to solidify his cult. In reality, the Torah and the Quran are completely different books, which venerate two wholly dissimilar deities. For those who may be unaware, the Quran itself makes no mention of the sacred ten commandments, and for whatever does bear the slightest resemblance, it distorts its interpretation to concoct *Sharia law*. In fact, Muhammad's lengthy career of debauchery and violence violates the Mosaic ten commandments entirely, and only proves that he was a false prophet.

Most importantly, it was Muhammad who believed that his self-proclaimed prophethood was legitimised by Hebrew tradition, and insisted that he was the *final* member of the Jewish line of prophets. There is one major flaw in his reasoning which casts immense scrutiny over the validity of Islam as the alleged original religion in history - there is absolutely no mention of *Islam* throughout the entire Bible.

THE BIBLE IS CORRUPT?

Any Muslim scholar will quickly act on reflex through years of indoctrination, and hastily claim by rote that the Bible, specifically the Torah (Tanahk), is the corruption of the Quran. This accusation derives back to Muhammad, who claimed that the Jews perverted the original Torah and its traditions, thus subsequently incurring the wrath of Allah. This explains why the god of the Arabs allegedly transformed one particular tribe of Israel into 'monkeys'.

> And you know well the story of those among you who broke Sabbath. We said to them:
> "Be apes—despised and hated by all."
> Quran 2:65

While Muslims will cling to this narrative, profusely insisting that the Torah today is the corruption of Allah's word, it is indeed the opposite which is true. Logically speaking, it is a foolish and bold claim to assert oneself as the original creator, when there is simply no proof for your contention. I've heard the 'Bible is corrupt' argument a thousand times, and even today, I'm still flawed by the lack of logical reasoning which Muslims evidently are unable to demonstrate. The most obvious rebuttal to the Muslim argument is the simple question:

If the Bible is corrupt, where is the original Islamic Torah and Injeel (Gospel)?

This question will always be met with distorted and angry faces from any Muslim firebrand, for the simple reason that there is no plausible explanation for both the books' disappearance. No true Muslim can deny the aforementioned tradition which makes an account of Muhammad swearing upon a book which at that time was allegedly uncorrupted. After all, why would the 'most perfect human' attest to a publication which might have been inherently fallible? Thus presents a double edged sword. Either Muhammad was a fool to swear upon a book which exposed his fraudulence, or that Allah allowed the 'uncorrupted' Torah to simply vanish. Such is the pitfall with lying.

Either answer condemns Islam and proves that its foundations are built on sand. If there is absolutely no proof of an original *Islamic* Torah ever having existed, then indeed Muhammad *did* jeopardise his prophethood, of which was already under immense scrutiny by his own inquisitive followers, *and* the Jews.

The issue of the Judaic Torah has always been a persistent bugbear for the Muslim nation. The fact that the book is still in existence, and by all accounts, still remains narratively corroborative and archaeologically accurate, leaves Islam open to vulnerabilities. Ask any Muslim the following questions, and be prepared to be met with askance looks.

Why has the original Islamic Torah conveniently disappeared?

And more importantly, why didn't Muhammad keep a copy to expose the Jews in the future?

Why did Allah allow the Jews to pervert his immutable and unchangeable word?

These are questions which Muslims will never dare answer, in fear of failing to form a rebuttal. It is abundantly obvious that Muhammad's egoism clouded his already poor judgment, as he quickly forgot one undeniable fact - the *illiterate* simpleton was unable to *read* the actual book he swore upon. How could an illiterate man know if the book he swore upon was 'corrupt' or not? In reality, even today he would not know the difference between a phone book or an actual Torah. Nonetheless, we can see that through this paradox that it is the Quran itself which is the corruption of God's word, and a cunning ploy by Muhammad to deceive mankind - simply put, there never has been an Islamic Torah.

If any Muslim were to contest this fact, I'm sure none will be able to explain how the 'Dead Sea Scrolls' predate Islam; these Jewish artefacts date back at least 150 B.C, which equates to over 700 years before Muhammad was born. Yet the Dead Sea Scrolls corroborate perfectly to the letter, and positively confirm that the Torah (Tanakh) has remained in a state of high authenticity and purity. Within the discovered manuscripts, 40% are copies of the Hebrew texts, while the rest are of non-canonised material. However, the scrolls verify completely that the Hebrew Torah is genuine. Nothing within the 23 books have changed.

Surely, any skeptic would insert a provocative notion to insinuate that the Jews were master collaborators in deception. But let's analyse the case logically. Surely, even the most proficient collective of Jewish brilliance could not be able to perfectly coordinate a fabrication without error; there would be trace elements of the corruption. Moreover, the actual geographical location of the scrolls is certainly condemning of Islam's claims, as the manuscripts were found in the Qumran caves - this being in the West bank (Palestine). If the texts were a fabrication, is is almost a certainty that they would not be located within the heart of Muslim territory. After all, Muslims claim that the West bank has always been Islamic land. It makes no sense why the scrolls would be placed within the heart of enemy land.

Furthermore, what is highly revealing, is that the 23 books written in the Tanakh correlate perfectly with each other, despite being composed in different eras, and in multiple locations, all by different authors. Yet none of the Tanakh's 23 books bear any resemblance to the Quran, or Islamic traditions. For what remains throughout the Quran, are various Judaic stories, all plagiarised, distorted and conflicting to the point of incoherency. If the Torah's narrative makes more sense than the Quran, how can any Muslim believe that the latter is the truth?

There are numerous changes to the Judaic narrative contained in the Quran. For example, according to Muhammad, Abraham was allegedly told to sacrifice Ishmael, not Isaac. But this is not possible as Hagar and her son were already exiled to the desert long before God made this testing commandment. Likewise, in the Quran, Noah's Ark finally lands on Mount Judi, while in the Bible it specifically says Mount Ararat. We know that accuracy leans toward the Torah, as Mount Ararat bears a physical outline of almost identical proportions to how the Ark is described in the Bible. Nonetheless, while these alterations might be trivial, they provide one question which Muslims can't answer…

What motivation would the Jews have to partially corrupt the original Islamic Torah, leaving variations of names and locations with the book?

By Muhammad's own contentions, it simply doesn't make sense. Logic would dictate that if the Jews were devious enough to erase history, they would have done so entirely. What would be the point in leaving large portions of the alleged Islamic narrative in their corrupted book, only to change names and locations? This loophole points an accusatory finger at Muhammad, which hints at the man himself plagiarising a foreign book and distorting *the* truth. Furthermore, if today's Torah can be traced back 2150 years to the original Mosaic texts at best, then it is ultimately the Quran which is the perversion of Torah. After all, the Quran was allegedly published only 1200 years ago. Without the original Islamic Torah to compare with, by default, the Quran is simply a corruption of God's word.

HAS ANYONE SEEN THE INJEEL?

Perhaps we should focus our attention on the fabled 'Injeel', otherwise known as the Islamic gospel; a book which Muhammad was also adamant existed.

According to Islamic sources, when Isa (Jesus) was born under a palm tree, Allah allegedly bestowed on him a book which was the confirmation of the Quran and Islam. This book, while widely referred to as 'the Injeel', is a misconstrued interpretation of the word 'gospel'.

> "And We sent, following in their footsteps, Jesus, the son of Mary, confirming that which came before him in the Torah; and We gave him the Injeel, in which was guidance and light and confirming that which preceded it of the Torah as guidance and instruction for the righteous."
> Quran 5:46

The fantastical telling of a baby Isa, who was allegedly and laughably able to speak like a man at birth, is not the only embarrassing tradition in the Islamic texts without merit. On the contrary, the Injeel, the crucial piece of the jigsaw puzzle to validate Muhammad's prophethood, has also conveniently been lost in history. What's condemning of Muhammad, is that not even he saw or touched this mythical book. It is obvious that his motivation to fabricate the existence of the fictitious book was to undermine the Christian faith, and especially their veneration for Jesus as God. Again, if something did not correlate with Islam, it *must be* corrupted in the eyes of Muhammad.

However, there is a gaping loophole in Muhammad's mendacious claim. Logic proves that if the Islamic Injeel actually existed, Allah would not require Muhammad to reveal the word of god once again; the Quran never states that the Injeel was corrupted. Therefore, the Injeel would indeed be entirely sufficient, and would be acceptable as a substitute for the Quran. This alone would invalidate Muhammad's life, who was allegedly called on by god to bring back 'the word' of god.

Why would Allah need Muhammad to correct an uncorrupted message? Surely, if the Injeel had disappeared as Muhammad claimed, it's almost guaranteed that someone would have preserved the book, or at least spread the message by oral tradition. As we can see throughout Islamic scripture, Allah's word was ultimately alien to the Meccan populous. Not one person was aware of the Injeel or 'the truth'. For a book which was allegedly delivered by god to a talking baby, it is highly revealing that history conveniently wiped clean the events of this miracle. Logically speaking, it only proves that Muhammad once again got caught in another lie, and never had the foresight to realise that the fabrication would damage his reputation. As we can see from within the Hadith, early Muslims were overly dependent on their prophet's word alone. No Muslim can deny that not even Muhammad could have witnessed the book, as he never *swore* upon it, and merely referred to it as legend. But alas, Muslims are forbidden to doubt their prophet - a crime punishable by death. And in effect, it is the pervasive fear of apostasy which has perpetuated the lie that is Muhammad.

As the Torah is able to be verified with the Dead Sea Scrolls, so is the New Testament (gospel) with the 'Codex Vaticanus' 300 A.D, the 'history of Flavius Josephus' 37-100 A.D, and the Annals of Roman historian, Senator Tacitus 58-117 A.D. The Codex Vaticanus proves without a doubt that every New Testament copy available today is of the highest authenticity. Furthermore, the testament of Josephus and Tacitus correlate perfectly with the Codex's narrative. Both authors predate the codex, and are wholly in agreement with the events that transpired in Judea, circa 33 A.D. From these books, we know that there was an individual from Nazareth who was known as Jesus, a son of a carpenter, who claimed to be God, who died and was resurrected, and was witnessed by thousands.

None of these authors could have gained anything by conspiring to create a myth. Josephus was a Jew, and not a Christian. Tacitus was a Roman pagan, whose career was not based in Judea. Furthermore, the authors of the Codex Vaticanus lived over 200 years after both the aforementioned authors died. All three wrote in different regions, all in different eras, and ascribed to entirely different faiths. Yet each author remained consistent and historically accurate in their accounts.

None of the aforementioned authors' testimonies are mentioned in the Quran, which is allegedly the derivative confirmation of the Injeel. The Quran itself emphatically rebukes the fact that Jesus was crucified, let alone resurrected.

> "And [for] their saying, "Indeed, we have killed the Messiah, Jesus, the son of Mary, the messenger of Allah ." And they did not kill him, nor did they crucify him; but [another] was made to resemble him to them. And indeed, those who differ over it are in doubt about it. They have no knowledge of it except the following of assumption. And they did not kill him, for certain."
> Quran 4:157

In the Islamic texts, Isa was simply a lowly prophet, who was inexplicably born through a virgin birth, yet was allegedly paving the way for an underwhelming, illiterate dwarf, who would suffer with multiple mental illnesses. This again only proves that the Quran is a fraudulent piece of literature. Not only by archaeological records, but by simple logic.

It's also undeniable that Muhammad never actually heard the true gospel in its entirety, and simply relied on fragmented and distorted oral traditions. Throughout the Quran, the New Testament's overtones are barely included. Furthermore, the Islamic codex bears no resemblance to any of the Christian epistles, their stories and the message of salvation. It's clear that most of Muhammad's teachings were firmly grounded on the Torah, which again is problematic for his claim of an Injeel ever existing. If Muhammad failed to include any New Testament story in the Quran, except the crucifixion (or the alleged non-event), it only proves that the man had no clue what he was talking about.

More puzzling is that Allah allegedly miraculously saved the lowly prophet Isa from the crucifixion, but inexplicably allowed the ultimate and most beloved messenger of Allah to die from poisoning. And at the same time, the god of Arabia also somehow managed to lose the one book which would exonerate Muhammad!

History dictates that empires have repeatedly attempted to destroy the Bible, and have ultimately failed. For what Muhammad alleged is a heretical corruption, the book has survived the worst. Evidently, the God of the Bible has preserved his word throughout the ages, but Allah is somehow found wanting. For a god whom Muhammad claimed to be the ultimate authority, he has a nasty habit of absentmindedly losing his prized possessions.

So why did Muhammad fabricate the story of the Injeel? Quite simply, after he heard vague stories of Jesus and the crucifixion - probably through his first wife Khadija's cousin Waraq, who was a cultural Christian - the man was desperate to quickly subsume the faith. Naturally, being the narcissist he was, he overshadowed Christianity, perverting it with Islam. After plagiarising immense portions of the Torah, he took whatever vague knowledge of the New Testament and forged the traditions into his faith. This time he borrowed themes, but not stories. Muhammad knew that to completely invalidate a faith which proved to be a direct threat to his suicidal cult, the necessity arose to undermine Christianity by claiming that Islam preceded all. He had already lied about an Islamic Torah, and he would need to fabricate the same myth to deal with Christians. By investing the legend of the Injeel, it would serve to confuse and entice followers to his organisation.

THE HELPER?

Today, there is a growing falsehood permeating throughout the Ummah, more so in the west, where a new mendacious narrative has formed regarding the New Testament. Without absolute evidence to prove the existence of Muhammad, Muslims have now resorted to flagrantly implying that the Biblical Jesus' foretelling of the holy spirit to come, 'the helper', is allegedly Muhammad.

> "But the Helper, the Holy Spirit, whom the Father will send in my name, he will teach you all things and bring to your remembrance all that I have said to you."
> John 14:26

The irony is that Muslims will denigrate the Bible as a corruption of the Quran, but are quick to refer to said 'corruption' to validate their ridiculous theories. Evidently, in an embarrassing move to save face from being outed as fools following the biggest fool in history, Muslim scholars have emulated their prophet's shortsightedness and completely sidestepped the subsequent events of the gospel, by omitting the Bible's Day of Pentecost. This momentous event of which

Jesus referred to as the advent of 'the helper', describes the holy spirit descending upon his disciples, bestowing upon them the gift of multi-regional linguistics.

Predictably, it is through Muslims' misunderstanding of New Testament scripture which has placed them in an untenable position to create such a ludicrous accusation that that 'the helper' is Muhammad. Again, the Quran's omission of this crucial turning point in the New Testament, only proves that Muhammad never completely heard the entire gospel, and imposed his ego to fill in the gaps to his flawed contentions. Thus for the last 1400 years, his followers have been placed in an awkward position to explain their master's flawed narrative.

While Muslims will still cling to 'the helper' urban legend, there is also another fact which condemns Islam. Nowhere in the entire New Testament, or in any Biblical prophetic vision, is the name *Muhammad* mentioned. As I have already explained, while Muhammad is not an actual name but a *title;* his name or title is completely exempt from the New Testament. If Allah had truly chosen a final prophet to come, surely his name would resound throughout the Bible, regardless if it is corrupt. Surely, regardless if the book is allegedly corrupt, the name Muhammad would have to be immutable, and incorruptible.

Even Muhammad himself promulgated the concept that his name could not be damaged, as the man narcissistically believed that the name *Muhammad* was impervious to criticism, ridicule or slander...

> "Doesn't it astonish you how *Allah* protects me from the Quraish's abusing and cursing? They abuse *Mudhammam* and curse *Mudhammam* while I am Muhammad (and not *Mudhammam*)."
> Sahih Bukhari 4:56:733

As I've already demonstrated, it was Muhammad who illogically believed Allah worshipped *him*, not the opposite. These are the tell tale signs of a man suffering with delusions of grandeur and a god complex. Nonetheless, as we can see, it seems that Muhammad was the new kid on the block, and desperately clung to the most available religions in that region, muscling in on their prophetic hierarchy.

A PROPHET WHO FULFILLED NO PROPHECIES

There are 66 books in the Bible. The entire compilation itself has been written by multiple authors, mostly in Israel, some while in lands as far away as Babylon, but *never* in Arabia. And yet, the books have correlated perfectly for over 3000 years. However, what Muslims cannot deny, is that none make any mention of Islam or specifically *Muhammad*. In *Revelation*, the last book of the Bible, neither is there any foretelling of a *final* prophet to come, or any prophet for that matter. According to the New Testament, the message is complete and all should expect Jesus the messiah to come again. There is no subtle nuance which could be interpreted as a prophecy for Muhammad's ascension, nor are there any historical loopholes which are so evidently displayed in Islamic history. Indeed, the entire book's narrative and prophetic message is flawless. What is written, is complete.

And while the Jews never did, and do not accept Jesus, the Tanakh's description of a coming Jewish messiah which predated Islam, bears no resemblance to Muhammad. Predominantly in the books of Genesis, Samuel, Zechariah, Psalms, Jeremiah, Daniel and Isaiah, there is an overwhelming theme of a *Jewish* messiah to come. However, if the Islamic world is still convinced that the Tanakh's premonitions of a Jewish saviour is Muhammad, I will outline the following prerequisites for the actual messiah in accordance with Biblical prophecy:

> He would be from the tribe of Judah (Jewish).
> Genesis 49:10 fulfilled in Matthew 1:1-16
> *Muhammad was an Arab, not a Jew.*
>
> He would be cut off from his own people, Israel.
> Isaiah 9:14, Daniel 9:26 fulfilled in Luke 4:14-30
> *Muhammad might have been expelled from his own people, but the verses relate to Israel.*
>
> He would be betrayed for 30 pieces of silver.
> Zechariah 11:12 fulfilled in Matthew 26:15
> *Muhammad was never betrayed by his followers for a sum of money.*
>
> He would be silent before his accusers.
> Isaiah 53:7 fulfilled in Mark 14:61
> *Muhammad was a boastful, vengeful man.*
>
> He would be spat on and scourged.

Isaiah 50:6 fulfilled in Matthew 26:67, John 19:1
Muhammad was never assaulted after fleeing to Medina. It was him who scourged and spat on people.

He would be executed with criminals.
Isaiah 53:12 fulfilled in Matthew 27:38
Muhammad was not executed. He died eventually from poison related complications.

His hands and feet would be pierced.
Psalm 22:16, Zechariah 12:10 fulfilled in Luke 23:33, John 20:25-27
Muhammad was never crucified, and never sustained physical injuries.

They would divide his clothes and cast lots.
Psalm 22:18 fulfilled in John 19:23-24
Muhammad was never taken prisoner or ridiculed before execution.

He would be crushed for our inequities.
Isaiah 53:5 fulfilled in Matthew 27:26, 29, Matthew 27:32-56
Muhammad lived a comfortable life raping, murdering and stealing. He sent others to their deaths, while watching from afar. He never sacrificed himself for the faith or mankind.

He would pray for his persecutors.

Isaiah 53:12 fulfilled in Luke 23:34
Muhammad cursed his enemies, and created homicidal war edicts to punish dissidents.

They would give him vinegar to drink.
Psalm 69:21 fulfilled in Matthew 27:33-34
Muhammad was never tortured or seized.

Taking all of these facts into consideration, I ask the reader, do these prophecies in anyway bear the slightest resemblance to *Muhammad?* Indeed, none of the major Biblical prophecies conform to Muhammad's recorded life in *Saudi Arabia*, which should be Israel. This again proves him to be a fraud.

Of course, any Muslim will predictably return to the 'Bible is corrupted' argument. However, what Muslims cannot deny is that Muhammad was neither Jewish, or from the line of Judah - *an important prerequisite for the messiah.* It was Muhammad who actually boasted of being an alleged descendent of Ishmael, Abraham's illegitimate son, instead of Isaac (for whom Jacob 'Israel' was begot), whom the God of the Bible chose.

But let's revisit the aforementioned prophecies in accordance with Muhammad's life. As we can see, the man certainly failed to meet the prerequisites for Biblical prophethood and the messiah. Muhammad lived a very comfortable life and was never persecuted in Medina, even until his death. He was never betrayed for any sum of money, let alone thirty pieces of silver, and would murder anyone who would insult him, more so if they spat on him. Muhammad was never silent before his accusers, and childishly returned the favour by equally mocking them. He was never pierced as punishment, never whipped, and neither was he executed. For anyone with a basic understanding of Jesus' final hours and crucifixion, it's blatantly obvious that these prophecies were not describing Muhammad.

THE MECCA PARADOX

There's no doubt that the Bible has become the inconvenient testament to the truth which Muslims are still plagued by today. As previously mentioned, the Quran and Islam is absent in two factors which the Bible bears - archaeologically and Biblical prophecy.

Unquestionably, every Biblical story has predominantly centred around Mesopotamia, Canaan, Israel and Egypt. Yet somehow the Islamic narrative inexplicably takes a u-turn into the Arabian peninsular. Furthermore, the Islamic Ka'aba, the house of worship which Muhammad was so infatuated over, is neither mentioned anywhere throughout the entire Bible. According to Muhammad, the Ka'aba is the most holiest site in Islam, which is inexplicably 1,500 km away from Jerusalem - of which the God of the Bible proclaimed to be *his* eternal city, not Mecca. No Muslim can ever explain why Muhammad, a gentile from Arabia, would find the necessity to commemorate an *idolatrous* house to the God of the Bible, in a distant land of the gentiles. Or why he would feel compelled to adorn blasphemous writings around its exterior. Blasphemies which deny the trinity, curse the Jews, and exalt Allah as the supreme deity. Again, if Muhammad was truly privy to *the* gospel as he claimed, he would have known that the God of the Bible comes in three persons, God, Son and Holy Spirit. Yet it was Muhammad who drove the misconception that Christians worship Jesus, Mary and Allah.

"And [beware the Day] when Allah will say, "O Jesus, Son of Mary, did you say to the people, 'Take me *and my mother as deities* besides Allah ?'" He will say, "Exalted are You! It was not for me to say that to which I have no right. If I had said it, You would have known it. You know what is within myself, and I do not know what is within Yourself. Indeed, it is You who is Knower of the unseen."
Quran 5:116

It's clearly evident through his irreverence and ignorance, that the man only briefly *heard* of the gospel, more specifically the crucifixion and nothing more. However, I strongly postulate that the original authors of the Quran, not the Hadith, were influenced by the Byzantine empire and Catholicism while in Syria. This again would preclude the notion that Islam originated from Mecca. How could any Meccan come to the misunderstanding that Christians worship Mary? This could only have happened if the Quran was written by people who were based near Constantinople - the new Rome. As you will soon learn in the following chapter, it is abundantly clear that *Syria* is most probably the location for the original authors of the Quran.

Regardless, when referring to the Hadith, we see that the latter authors of Islam penned accounts of Muhammad embroiled in pagan acts which would have offended the God of the Bible. The abhorrent pagan rituals conducted by the Meccans, detail the clan incessantly running around the Ka'aba naked. The fact that early Meccans would allegedly worship in the nude, while performing hysterical compulsive rituals, brought me to one conclusion. In my first book, I deduced that Muhammad's tribe, the Quraysh, were a fertility cult, engaging in ritualistic orgies which lead to Muhammad's syphilis at age 40. Fertility cults were very common in ancient times, and invariably involved communal sexual practices, to commemorate either Dionysus or Artemis. Surely, these abominable pagan rituals would be completely incompatible with the God of the Torah he swore upon.

A FLAWED RELIGION FOR A FLAWED PROPHET

Considering the innumerable plot holes in Muhammad's bloated account, Muslims have for 1400 years attempted to create a cohesive narrative, but always fail egregiously. Indeed, Islam is *the* band-aid religion. Whenever there is inconsistency, Muslims apply the *band-aid* of irrationality to coverup the flaws, only to create a whole new tangent of questioning which inevitably condemns their faith. One can understand why there is so much confusion today in the Islamic world.

Despite the incessant accusations Muslims will throw at critics to malign their findings, there is one irremovable fact that remains - there is no mention of *Islam* throughout the entire Bible. And regardless that Muslims believe that the book is allegedly corrupted, not even the entire Ummah will concede that the *whole* book is perverted. Alas, shades of Judaic traditions remain in the Quran, which only proves Muhammad believed that *not all of the book* was contaminated.

From this, it certainly validates that either Muhammad fabricated the entire backstory of Islam based on his vague understanding of Judaism, or that he never existed. For the latter, it's more plausible that the Persian scholar Bukhari created a fictional character, and filled in the Quran's overwhelming gaps by blaming the Jews for perverting the 'original' Quran.

It's very easy to coverup one's own transgressions by conveniently insinuating that the victim destroyed the evidence, especially when the victim is prohibited to testify with hard proof. If our laws were based on such irrationality, prisons would remain underpopulated. But alas, the accusatory offensive of Muslims is the predictable retort 'the Jews corrupted the word'. This mantra has continued to glue the cult together for 1400 years. If Islam was the one true faith, surely Allah himself would have preserved some form of evidence long before the birth of Muhammad. And since the Injeel has conveniently disappeared, this too also proves Allah to be either feckless or a fraud.

To claim that one man alone was suddenly burdened with the task of ending an age old Jewish conspiracy to bury the truth, is an absurd notion. Truth is truth. And no matter how hard someone tries to suppress it, the truth will always reveal itself. Truth is immutable, and it doesn't need an illiterate man to reveal it once again. If we are to rely on the word of a man who was repeatedly found wanting in his illogical argument, then Islam is ultimately a lie.

WHY IS THERE NO PROOF MECCA EXISTED IN ANCIENT TIMES?

To debunk Islam, it is crucial to hone in our investigation directly on the issue of Mecca - the alleged town where Muhammad was born; the birthplace of Islam. Undeniably, Mecca is by far *the* most important factor within Islamic tradition. We know this because in Islamic law, it is obligatory for *every* Muslim to complete the 'hajj' pilgrimage at least once in their lifetime; a journey which takes them back to the origins of the faith and to pay observance to a *box* and a *black stone*. As the city itself has long been regarded as the most holiest site in Islam, for obvious reasons, it is axiomatic that Mecca is the crucial linchpin for the faith. However, there is one slight problem with Mecca…

There is absolutely no proof it existed during and before Muhammad's time.

The proposition that such a crucial landmark in Islam is the figment of someone's imagination, is a controversial concept that Muslims will undoubtedly and automatically rebuke as anathema. As Islam is no doubt a cult, their contentions are solidly grounded in the traditions of Muhammad and his teachings. Whatever *he* said became truth, immaterial of opposing facts.

There is an old saying in Islam which has served to underpin mendacious Islamic legends which prevent Muslims from ever accepting what is evident:

> "Just because you can't see it, doesn't mean it's not there."
>
> - Old Arabic proverb

But it is within that foolish and obstinate mindset which opens up Islam to speculation, as the faith is exempt of concrete proof or basic logic. Sadly for Islam, Mecca's alleged historicity is without either, and is more akin to fable instead of fact.

THE MECCAN TRINITY PARADOX

As Islamic legend dictates, Muhammad was irremovably and firmly sold on the concept that Mecca's Ka'aba (the Islamic house of worship) was built by Abraham and his son Ishmael. But it is Muhammad's irrational statement which opens Islam up to a number of questions. One may wonder how Abraham and Ishmael actually ended up in Mecca, especially when the God of the Bible had commanded the father of many nations to dwell specifically in 'Canaan' - 1500 km's away. As the Bible details in Genesis 21:8-20, Abraham's wife made her husband expel his maidservant Hagar, and his illegitimate firstborn son, Ishmael. According to the subsequent scriptures, the maidservant apparently crossed the desert of Beersheba with a single skin of water, before the angel of the Lord saved her from death by guiding her to a well.

In contrast with Islamic tradition, the Biblical account is far more tangible regarding geographical and logical terms. However, according to Muhammad's claims, Hagar's expulsion resulted in her and Ishmael traversing the *Arabian* desert, not Beersheba. Similarly to the Bible, mother and son survived on a single skin of water, but inexplicably and successfully managed to travel 1500 km's south through the wilderness, before eventually running out of water. Logistically speaking, her trip would have taken *months*, if successful. However, we can see that the plagiaristic nature of Muhammad lends itself to the story, as the tradition holds that an Islamic angel miraculously guided Hagar to a well, which is known today as the 'Zam-Zam well'. This key Islamic tradition is *the* foundation of Mecca's existence, as it was Hagar who allegedly founded the ancient city. As Muhammad dictated, it was then that Abraham travelled to Mecca from 'Syria' on a flying donkey, to build the Ka'aba, for reasons unknown. Each day, it is alleged that Abraham would fly back to Syria on his magic donkey, attending to his first wife, much like a travelling salesman. While this tradition will no doubt be a source of ridicule for people with an IQ over 85, there are still a number of problems in Muhammad's theory.

What is baffling, is that there is absolutely no archaeological proof of any individuals resembling the three aforementioned characters ever existing in Mecca. There are no engravings, no monuments venerated to them, no coins… nothing. Neither is there any literature or artistic representation recording the miraculous 'Buraq', i.e flying donkey. Secondly, Abraham was unquestionably buried in *Canaan*, i.e Israel, not Mecca. Anyone can visit his tomb today in Hebron, which is a source of great contention for the Judaic and Islamic schism. Inevitably, there's two separate issues with this revealing fact which will confound Muslims till no end.

Why was Abraham buried in 'Israel', when his mandate was to build Mecca, especially when he was allegedly from Syria?

If Mecca took precedent in Islamic geographical importance, why is the grandfather of Islam buried in Israel (the homeland of the Jews), and not Syria?

ARCHAEOLOGICALLY AND LOGICALLY UNSOUND

According to the Bible, when Abraham died, Ishmael actually attended the funeral with his half brother Isaac to bury their father. Semitic culture dictates that burials occur within 24 hours. However, the conundrum that lies within Islamic tradition is that Ishmael was purported to be living in Mecca during that time. How could Ishmael allegedly return to his father's homeland within 24 hours - on foot?! Does Islam claim that Isaac travelled 1500km's in one day? Even by Islamic standards, it's impossible as the tradition holds that Ishmael never had access to his father's flying donkey. Believe me, I have scoured all available sources regarding this story - none describe any account of Ishmael being privy to such supernatural creatures.

The Abraham-Ishmael saga is ultimately an incredulous story so full of holes that it would make any hardened detective suspicious. For what we can ascertain, the plagiarised story of 'Hagar' and Islam's inexplicable, geographically confused tradition, was amalgamated to tie in with Muhammad's desperate claim to Jewish prophethood. According to Islamic history, the Meccans eventually embraced idolatry and paganism, and venerated all different gods and idols - 360 in observance, to be exact. Considering that the Meccans, hundreds of years later, were allegedly all encompassing of faiths and never discarded any idols, it is highly feasible that these alleged peoples must have kept some form of commemoration to the original creators of the Ka'aba. Yet there is no record of Abraham, Hagar or even Ishmael ever existing in that area. No archaeologist has ever found an idol depicting the Meccan trinity. Naturally, one might suspect that any Muslim would have destroyed such artefacts, but this only proves that Muslims would prefer to shoot themselves in the foot, rather than verifying their religion's origins. Still, there is no Islamic tradition in the Hadith which details any Muslim discovering such artefacts and acknowledging graven evidence of the patriarch, wife and their issue.

Consequently, fabricated genealogy is the only direct connection Muhammad claimed to have with the aforementioned trio. And as we can see from the texts, it was Muhammad who vehemently propagated the lie that *he* was the direct descendent of Ishmael, an alleged fact that he was most proud of. But again, regardless of the absence of physical proof, there is still no historical record of that name ever existing in Arabia before Muhammad's alleged existence. Neither is there any derivative etymological names confirming this fact. It seems that Judaic culture never really existed in Mecca. In fact, it was only after Muhammad emigrated to Medina that he became absorbed in Hebrew tradition, after mingling with the three main Jewish tribes. If that is the case, why does the Islamic world profess that a town 500 km's away to the south of Medina, takes top priority within the Biblically themed Quran? Again, this is simply illogical.

WHICH KA'ABA IS IT, MUHAMMAD?

Concerning the issue of the Ka'aba, there is an inherent problem that exists with Muslims' claims that the edifice we know today is *the* actual Mosque during Muhammad's era. As previously mentioned, Muhammad mistakenly believed that Abraham had built *one* exclusive house to commemorate Allah, the 'Al-Masjid Al-Haram'. Even today, Muslims also cling to the belief that the location of this historically described Mosque validates the existence of ancient Mecca. To begin with, the word 'Ka'aba' is actually a universal term, and not exclusive to one single structure. The definition itself could be equated to 'a

Mosque' instead of *The* Mosque of Allah'. In fact, the word simply means 'cube' and refers to any *cubed* structure used by pagans before the advent of Islam. While Muslims will vehemently rebuke this fact, the truth remains inside the Islamic texts, of which they cannot deny.

Indeed, the Hadith and ancient Islamic texts explicitly demonstrate that there were at least three other 'cubed' structures in existence during Muhammad's time!

In the book of Sahih Muslim 31:6052, the text describes the existence of a temple called 'Dhu'l-Khalasah', which was referred to as the Yemenite Ka'aba, or the northern Ka'aba. Likewise, the Islamic author Diwan al-A'sha penned and account of another Ka'aba which was venerated by the tribe of al-Harith Ibn-Ka'b in the area of Najran. Finally, the book of Sifah also details a third Ka'aba in the region of Sindad, located between al-Kufah and al-Basrah.

Surely, these facts alone contradict Muhammad's assertion that there was only *one* Ka'aba in existence. The verifiable existence of these pagan houses of worship cast immense doubt on Muhammad's claims and the alleged existence of ancient Mecca.

Furthermore, the 'Qibla' in Islam is the word which signifies the *direction* of worship for all Mosques in the world, which is always to be towards Mecca. In Islam, this is irremovable, and the cornerstone of Muslims' worship. However, in the British Channel 4 documentary "Islam - the untold story", investigators proved that the most earliest Mosques did not face towards Mecca. One particular archaeological remnant of a mosque in eastern Israel, was demonstrated to have faced towards the east, but never Mecca, which would have been towards the south. And yet, the mosque in question was apparently built centuries after Muhammad died. Again, this only proves that hundreds of years after Muhammad's reign, not even the Qibla was determined; ergo Mecca was hastily written into the Islamic texts as a stop-gap. While the Quran only mentions the word 'Ka'aba' three times, this would only bolster the fact that the book's description is ultimately ambiguous, as it never nominates a specific geographical location for where it stands. Unequivocally, the Hadith actually makes mention of the edifice far more than the Quran. And as we have learned, the subsequent codex supersedes the Quran by at least 200 years.

BACA OR MACORABA?

In actuality, never is the name 'Mecca' listed throughout the 104 books in the Quran. Instead, the only resemblance to the name Mecca, is 'Baca', which again gives no clear insight to any geographical location in Arabia. In fact, while the name Baca is actually written in the Biblical Old Testament, it is specifically described as a route towards Jerusalem from a *northern* passage of Lebanon - never towards the south from Arabia. As the Bible describes:

> "Blessed are those whose strength is in you, who have set their hearts on pilgrimage. As they pass through the Valley of Baca, they make it a place of springs: the autumn rains also cover it with pools. They go from strength to strength, till each appears before God in Zion... Better is one day in your courts than a thousand elsewhere; I would rather be a doorkeeper in the house of my God than dwell in the tents of the wicked."
> Psalm 84:4-7, 10

> "Once more the Philistines came up and spread out in the Valley of Rephaim; so David inquired of the LORD, and he answered, 'Do not go straight up, but circle around behind them and attack them in front of the balsam (Hebrew- Baca) trees.'"
> 2 Samuel 5:22-23

This demonstrates that the Quran's Baca is far removed from the Biblical description. The actual valley of Baca is only five miles from Jerusalem, not 1500 km's away, as Mecca is today. Of course, the distinct lack of proof that Baca is the actual Mecca has caused a maelstrom in the Islamic academic world. Nonetheless, Muslims are somewhat incapable of dealing with the truth and still insist that the name Baca is accurate, regardless of the facts.

Thus, the inescapable lack of proof regarding Mecca's historical non-existence has now provoked Muslim scholars to desperately comb western historical archives, frantically attempting to find an alternative form of proof to validate Muhammad's claim. For some time, Islamic scholars have clung to a misconception over the historical recording of a town called 'Macoraba', discovered by the Roman 'Claudius Ptolemy', who lived from 100-170 A.D. It's staggering to see that even today, there are thousands of publications which have bought into the lie that Macoraba is Mecca. It's a lazy form of research, where authors have carelessly based their work on unsubstantiated claims, undoubtedly to conform with politically correct standards in fear of the Islamic world erupting. But the facts are far more confronting, and inescapably disprove the cult's claims.

In a thesis written by researcher Dan Gibson, titled "Suggested solutions for issues concerning the location of Mecca in Ptolemy's geography", Gibson analysed Ptolemy's detailed charter of the middle-east, by applying the ancient historian's coordinates as a transparent overlay on the Saudi Arabian map. His findings trumped modern historians and their publications:

> "We then decided to place Ptolemy's coordinates on a grid without any reference to any maps. Then we would try and match the rivers to see what Ptolemy had done. When we attempted to overlay these coordinates on a modern map many problems arose when trying to fit them correctly."
> - Dan Gibson

Conclusively, Gibson's work proved that the 'Macoraba' which academics and the Islamic world have erroneously referred to as Mecca, is an entirely different city in a distant region. In fact, the Encyclopaedia of Religion and Ethics, in, Vol. 8, p.511, states that the name is of an entirely alternate linguistic root than Mecca. How academics have overlooked this fact, truly boggles the mind.

A HISTORICAL TRADING HUB?

Furthermore, there is also the issue of recorded historical, commercial trading in the southern Arabian region which again throws doubt on Mecca's existence. Regardless if modern historians are obstinately opposed to shifting their opinion, ancient archives prove that there has *never* been any significant trade route through a city called Mecca. According to whoever penned early Islamic history, Mecca was allegedly a thriving commercial hub, home to a mercantile trading tribe known as 'the Quraysh'. But again, there is no historical records to validate these alleged native peoples. Neither is there any archaeological evidence.

If Mecca was indeed the bustling commercial hub early Islamic historians had described, then trade routes would be significantly easy to trace through ancient archives, predominantly according to the Roman empire's mercantile records. But again, there is no tangible proof of a renowned trade route exceeding the empire's borders as far as Mecca. In fact, for whatever ancient historical archives are in existence, which detail civilizations in the southern Arabian peninsular, there are more detailed accounts of the 'Queen of Saba', or Sheba, who was a monarch of Yemen - 1000 km's south of Mecca. Surely, if Muhammad's contention that the ancient Meccans eclipsed the Yemeni kingdom, ancient historians would certainly have celebrated its mercantile prowess over all hubs within that region. Alas, there is still no record, and the ancient Queen's reputation still overshadows Mecca's alleged existence.

Assuredly, even throughout the ancient Queen's illustrious career as the dominant force in the region, there would be some record of surrounding trading hubs, including Mecca. Admittedly, whatever records of the monarch once existing, have unfortunately disappeared in time - all except from the Bible. In fact, the book makes a candid account of the Queen herself who allegedly traversed with her entourage to Israel to pay homage to King Soloman, who both subsequently bore a child. If the Bible itself, which is apparently a corruption of the Quran, details the existence of an ancient Queen in neighbouring Yemen, then why is Mecca forgotten?

THE KHADIJA PARADOX

Within the Meccan conundrum, there is also the gaping loophole in Islamic historicity which is Muhammad's first wife, Khadija. According to the texts, his consort was regarded as the daughter of a powerful trading magnate who was recorded to have actually disapprovingly called Muhammad 'a bum'. This tradition is very telling, as it shows that not even Muhammad, the self-proclaimed master of the universe, was up to snuff to marry the daughter of a trade merchant in an obscure town. From what is written in Tabari's 'History', we can deduce that Khadija's father was tantamount to Donald Trump, and was of immense importance to the region. Naturally, after her father died, Khadija inherited his commercial empire, and subsequently bankrolled the cult.

Nonetheless, what can be agreed is that Khadija's reputation for shrewd mercantile prowess was unrivalled, and was the alleged backbone of the Meccan trading industry. We must also recognise that Muhammad never worked again from age 25, and depended on his wife to support him. Considering that her reputation would have eclipsed Muhammad's for many years, it leaves one gaping loophole in Islamic history - there is no mention of her in any secular account regarding ancient trade contacts. The woman is a ghost, and only exists in the esoteric and obscure annals of Islamic biographies. Again, I have scoured all available ancient sources regarding ancient middle-eastern contracts, and no scribe in Roman history has recorded this woman, or the resemblance of her. This is highly condemning of Islam, as we know that her legacy of trading was dynastic to say the least. Yet, not even her father or kin are mentioned in any notable imperial trading archives. The whole Meccan dynasty is vacuous.

Surely, even the most hardcore Muslim firebrand would find this peculiar, and must concede that hints of Muhammad's creators' mendacity had resulted in her family's fictionalisation.

AN EMPTY SHOP

The issue of Mecca's alleged time-sensitive flora and agriculture is also a confronting fact which will puzzle the most knowledgeable Muslim on Islam. In the Quran and the Hadith, the species of trees described are 'olives', which were allegedly in abundance in Mecca long before Muhammad was born. Islamic tradition describes a rich oasis, replete in vegetation, for which an agrarian society was apparently able to flourish. There's a slight problem with this case - there are no olive tree plantations in Mecca, and never has there been. The Mecca today is chiefly known to contain mostly date trees.

Again, this would lead scholars to deduce that the early Quran was written around *Syria,* especially considering the aforementioned fantastical tales of Abraham and Hagar. Most notably, Syria has been historically known for its olive trees, and is widely referred to as the birthplace of the species. No ancient historian or traveler of significant repute has made any recording of any plantation growing in southern Arabia, let alone olive trees. It's therefore unknown what the alleged illustrious Quraysh tribe were able to trade with, especially if these plantations were non-existent. Without agriculture, the Quraysh would consequently be exempt from trading in textiles, dyes, or fruit produce - the primary exports in that time. The economic ramifications of a stagnant and retrograde outpost would consequentially result in an imminent demise long before Muhammad was born. Simply put, there is no way Mecca could have existed. It would have been doomed from the start.

WHY DOES MECCA EXIST TODAY?

But how can we explain the existence of Mecca today if it never existed before? Very simply, Bukhari's mendacious and conniving initiatives created a domino effect, and a cultural vacuum which has driven Muslims by compulsion to travel to a fabled land. By creating the fifth pillar of Islam, where all Muslims are mandatorily required to visit the Ka'aba at least once in their lifetime, the entire Islamic world has flocked to a mythological destination to bolster the lie. Ironically, it's crucial to note that the *location* where Muslims must travel to for the Hajj pilgrimage is *never* mentioned in the entire Quran. The closest tradition which alludes to it is…

> "When you disperse from Arafat you shall commemorate God at the Mishaar Al-Haram."
> Quran 2:198

But by all accounts, this verse is the sole tradition which allegedly prescribes all Muslims to visit Mecca. Anyone can see that the writ is ambiguous, at best. The name Mishaar al-Haram is wholly unidentifiable and inconclusive. Today, Islamic scholars have tried to bolster the argument that the name indicates a geographical location, namely a mountain. Yet the issue has still remained unresolved. In fact, the only time where the word 'Hajj' was written in detail, is in the Hadith - which was written 230 years after Muhammad died! Likewise, the name 'Mecca' however only appears similarly in the Hadith, not the Quran. From these two facts, it is evident that Bukhari had written his fictitious account in an attempt to reconcile fallacious Islamic history together with the Quran, in a semi-coherent fashion. As we have already discovered, the amount of plot holes in Islamic history which remains, is overwhelmingly staggering.

Clearly, it is evident that Mecca has become akin to the fabled Atlantis. Today, the city may as well be an Islamic Disneyland, or a Muslim Graceland. A destination for fans to revel in the cultural attractions, visit landmarks, gift shops, and to play cosplay dress-up in accordance with the traditions. After all, Mecca today has become somewhat of a tourist trap, and nothing more. The Saudi government has heavily invested in turning the city into a theme park of sorts, where large hotels dominate the skyline, and mega malls are planted next to the Ka'aba.

As I noted in my first book, this commercialisation of alleged hallowed ground would actually please Muhammad. The deliberate incorporation of pagan worship and Ramadan (lunar cycle observance) drove immense wealth into the city, as all were compelled by Islamic code to spend during the 'sacred months'.

ANY MECCA WILL DO

Axiomatically, for all intents and purposes it was a crucial necessity for those who wrote Islamic history to nominate an area in Arabia, which was far from being densely populated. To choose a barren wasteland, a blank canvas, would extricate historians from culpability, as there would be no trace evidence or geographical landmarks in southern Arabia to conflict with their stories. They simply made it up as they went. Thus the legend perpetuated itself, as pilgrims were quick to nominate certain key locations in a desperate attempt to bind the Islamic myth together. One can imagine the mad dash to 'name it and claim it', when assigning locales such as Muhammad's house, or even the Zam Zam well.

Likewise, the echelon most certainly would have commissioned the discovery of sacred artefacts, regardless of their authenticity. These being Muhammad's shoes, teeth, beard, or whatever they could fabricate. The truth was not important. After all, the Arabs were forging a religious empire based on a myth. The *truth* would only get in the way of their agenda. And thus, the entire Islamic fable has materialised through chronic dogmatism, embellishments and outright lying.

In fact, early Islamic historians are the sole culprits in mythologizing a middle-eastern theatre where an alleged prophet was born in a fictitious town known as Mecca, or Baca. Islamic history has remained esoterically understood, devoid of truth, and mired in conspiracy for 1400 years. Sadly, even big name publishers such as Encyclopaedia Britannica, and many other once reputable sources, have buckled under pressure to propagate the lie which is Islam. I challenge the reader to visit any library in the west, and research the topic of Mecca. All resources and archives will mendaciously advocate the myth that the Mecca in Saudi Arabia existed for over 2000 years, and is allegedly substantiated. There is an extensive list of authors who are deserving of censure and to be placed in the literature hall of shame for propagating the lie that is Mecca. Some of these have been renowned professors, and even Christian clergymen. Whether their work was penned under delusion, general intimidation by society's growing standards steeped in Islamism, or radical liberalism, the facts are evident - political correctness has forced once reputable publications, authors and historians to lie under pressure.

Yet the truth remains immutably confronting - Mecca certainly never existed during Muhammad's lifetime. Indeed, Islamic history can only be described as wildly abstract. It exists only in idea, instead of what is concrete. However, there is truly only one word to describe Muslims' misguided belief in a religion that fails time and time again to provide facts over fantasy. That word is 'indoctrination'.

But please, don't take my word as gospel. Recently deceased Patricia Crone, former professor of Islamic and Arab studies at the University of Princeton, lead a constructive discourse into the divisive conclusions that Islamic history is too vague to be taken seriously.

> "You cannot reject the Muslim story, but you cannot accept it either. The only solution is to step out of Islamic tradition and start again."
> Patricia Crone, P.H.D

For a woman who had dedicated her life to unravelling the mystery that is Islam, not even she herself could attest to the religion's alleged veracity. While I won't speak on her behalf, I will say this: Mecca is a lie.

IF THE QURAN IS INCORRUPTIBLE, WHY WERE THE EARLY COPIES DESTROYED?

It cannot be denied that Muslims hold up the Quran as a badge of honour, stating that the book has never been corrupted since the beginning of time. Yes, you read correctly. Islam teaches that the book has always existed, co-eternally with Allah, yet obviously contextually varied since its alleged state of omnipotence, considering that Muhammad was born in 570 and mandated to correct mankind. However, the 'message' allegedly has remained unchanged, and has apparently always proclaimed that Islam has been the original religion. One can understand why Muslims fervently adore and adulate a book that is regarded by the Ummah to be petrified in eternal 'truth', transcending the boundaries of time.

If the Quran is allegedly *the* ultimate, then everything else must pale in comparison. And most importantly, all other Biblical texts *must* be the corruption of God's word. Thus is the Muslim logic, bolstered by a narcissistic man, feigning to be a 'prophet'. Moreover, the fact that the Bible exists today in multiple versions, also has remained a source of inexplicable ridicule for Muslims, motivating them to malign and attack Judeo-Christianity as a perversion of Islam. In the eyes of a Muslim, the Quran has *never* been corrupted, nor necessarily translated into multiple versions. Ask any Muslim, and I assure you this is the rhetoric they will propagate.

However, it's predictable that the Ummah would jump to such an impulsive conclusion to believe that the multiple Biblical versions are entirely incompatible. Quite simply, all Muslims are strongly discouraged from actually reading any Bible, and thus are unable to verify their own claims. In truth, it's rare that any Muslim would dare read a page from the Bible, even while living in the west, as the trend of severe censorship was promulgated specifically by Muhammad, who narcissistically rebuked anyone who dared to read it.

> "Umar brought a copy of the Torah to the Prophet and said: "O Apostle of God, this is a copy of the Torah." But the Prophet kept silent. Then Umar started reading and the face of the Prophet kept changing. So, Abu Bakr interrupted him violently: "Don't you see the face of the Prophet?" Umar looked at the Prophet's face and said "May God preserve me from his anger..."
> Then the Prophet said: "If Moses appeared to you and you followed him and left me, you would go astray from the right path and if he were alive he would have followed me."
> Sunan ad-Darimi

What Muslims fail to realise is that the Bible's multiple versions are simply translations written in various grammatical *styles*. The overwhelming narrative and context remain unchanged. Only the *delivery* of writing differs from old english to contemporary. However, I am referring to *the* Bible, Sola Scriptura, not the Apocrypha, nor the Mormon or Jehovah's witness texts. Yet Muslims are largely unaware of these sects. I'm specifically talking about *the* book which predates civilization, spanning back as far as 1000 B.C, as opposed to the 1300 year old Quran. This is a relevant fact which you will soon realise the importance of.

I'm sure you might have heard the pervasive Muslim accusation that "the Bible is so corrupted because they make new ones ever year." As far as I know, there has only been one Bible, which was translated perfectly from the King James version.

This Muslim argument has no doubt been fuelled by their Imams who will take fiction, and turn it into fact. Muslims are master of non-sequiturs, and will quickly resort to fallacy as a diversionary tactic to conceal the truth.

THE QURAN HAS REMAINED UNCHANGED?

But as always, like many Muslim arguments, it's the pot calling the kettle black. The claim that the Quran is unilaterally equal with all copies, and without differentiation, is entirely false. The glaring irony is that in terms of 'translation', the Quran itself is no different. We know this as there are 11 translated versions of the book - a fact that Muslims conveniently omit from argument. Objectively speaking, like the Bible, each translation remains largely identical to its kin. Nonetheless, I challenge the reader to ask any Muslim about their Quran, specifically about its alleged perpetual state of authenticity. The reaction would be predictably banal, and boilerplate in terms of Muslim rebuttals. I guarantee that answers will be similar to this statement…

"It's never been corrupted, unlike your Bible. The Quran has remained unchanged ever since Muhammad revealed Allah's word. There is no proof it has been contaminated."

Of course, if the reader is still not convinced, the following is a list of quotes from Islamic authorities insisting on the Quran's veracity, and its infallibility.

The Quran is the speech from Allah, revealed in its precise meaning and wording through the angel Gabriel, transmitted by many, inimitable, unique and protected by Allah Himself against any corruption. (Ahmad Von Denffer, `Ulum Al-Qur'an, Leicester: The Islamic Foundation, 1994 (Revised edition), p. 21)

The Quran was memorised by Mohammed and then dictated to his companions, and written down by scribes, who cross-checked it during his lifetime. Not one word of its 114 chapters (suras) have ever been changed over the centuries. (Understanding Islam and the Muslims, The Australian Federation of Islamic Councils Inc. (pamphlet) Nov. 1991)

The text of the Quran is entirely reliable. It has been as it is, unaltered, unedited, not tampered with in any way, since the time of its revelation. (M. Fethullah Gulen, Questions this Modern Age Puts to Islam, London: Truestar, 1993, p.58)

There are literally hundreds of other Muslim quotations vehemently defending the incorruptibility of Allah's book. But by all accounts, we now have discovered a vulnerability which undoubtedly would see Islam come crashing down based on the simple fact - the Quran *has* indeed been changed, by none other than Muhammad's follower, 'Uthman'.

Let us begin...

AN EMBARRASSING FIASCO

There is an obscure tradition contained in the Islamic texts which is a source of embarrassment for Muslims today, and has remained so for centuries. However, there are hardly any Muslims who are aware of the following historical blunder, and those who do know, callously conceal the truth out of shame. By far, this tradition is the proverbial straw which will break the camel's back. Thus, the following tradition will prove that Muslims' knowledge today is devoid of historical accuracy, and founded on false bravado.

While the Hadith does state Muhammad did not possess one unique Quran, but in fact many, we can deduce that the compilation of these codices formed what was universally known as the first Quran. However, there were certain incidences where followers had versions which varied from each other, perhaps to the point of ostensible incoherency…

> Narrated Umar bin Al-Khattab: I heard Hisham bin Hakim reciting Surat Al-Furqan during the lifetime of Allah's Apostle and I listened to his recitation and noticed that he recited in several different ways which Allah's Apostle had not taught me. I was about to jump over him during his prayer, but I controlled my temper and when he had completed his prayer, I put his upper garment around his neck and seized him by it and said, "Who taught you this Surat which I heard you reciting ?" He replied, "Allah's Apostle taught it to me". I said, "You have told a lie, for Allah's Apostle

taught it to me in a different way from yours". So I dragged him to Allah's Apostle and said, "I heard this person reciting Surat Al-Furqan in a way which you haven't taught me!" On that Allah's Apostle said, "Release him (Umar) recite, O Hisham!" Then he recited in the same way I heard him reciting. Then Allah's Apostle said, "It was revealed in this way", and added, "Recite, O Umar", I recited it as he had taught me. Allah's Apostle then said, "It was revealed in this way. This Qur'an has been revealed to be recited in seven different ways, so recite of it whichever is easier for you."
Sahih Bukhari 6:61:514

However, what can be universally agreed upon, is that the Qurans available during Muhammad's lifetime, were *somewhat* in complete concordance and correlation. Furthermore, it is also widely acknowledged that the many pieces forming the first authorised Quran were eventually coherent to the point of authenticity to make only *one* copy.

As legend has it, not long after the death of Muhammad, the Quran was quickly distributed throughout the Islamic empire in written form. However, as the text was widely disseminated, greater the variations became. And over time, what was considered to be a perfect rendition was eventually *corrupted*. At one point the entire codex became so dissimilar, that no Quran bore any resemblance to the original, or with each other. None were able to reconcile with Islamic tradition, which caused immense tension and schisms throughout the land. Just imagine, the entire theocracy which had based its foundations on *one* book, had become jeopardised by systemic corruption of the word. This embarrassing fiasco was enough to provoke violent confrontations over the text and cast major doubts over the Qurans' alleged authenticity.

WHEN IN DOUBT, BURN IT?

If we further refer to the Hadith, the incident is described in vivid detail. The epic fallout of such a scandal caused the Islamic empire to implode, almost to the point of collapse. As there was no way to determine which book was the true copy, desperate measures were initiated lest the caliphate dissolve. To conceal the lie, the early Muslims resorted to an act of impulsivity to save face, and consequently, this tradition indelibly ruined the Quran's purported reputation for accuracy and incorruptibility.

However, whether the following accounts even occurred is debatable, considering Bukhari's nefarious intentions to rewrite history of his own accord. Nonetheless, we must base our argument on what is actually recorded and considered holy writ. While the following tradition is quite extensive, I have abbreviated the text for clarity's sake…

> "In case you disagree with Zaid bin Thabit on any point in the Qur'an, then write it in the dialect of Quraish, the Qur'an was revealed in their tongue." They did so, and when they had written many copies, 'Uthman returned the original manuscripts to Hafsa. 'Uthman sent to every Muslim province one copy of what they had copied, and ordered that

all the other Qur'anic materials, whether written in fragmentary manuscripts or whole copies, be burnt."
Sahih Bukhari 6:61:510

As you can see, the caliphate had reached a fever pitch over this embarrassing debacle, and had resorted to the ancient form of a *paper-shredding* to cover up the truth. Ultimately, Uthman ordered that every last copy of the Quran be burned, except one. Not only does this embarrassing situation truly condemn the validity of Islam, it also opens up the faith to a barrage of scrutiny and the ominous presence of questions which can't be answered.

The most resounding of all...

How did Uthman himself know he had the one true Quran?

Considering that there would have been innumerable copies of dissimilar texts, any Muslim must admit that verification would be impossible. Moreover, why didn't Uthman verify the Quran with the original scriptures which were allegedly carved into bones and written on palm fronds? As we can see from the aforementioned verse, Uthman completely side-stepped this authentication process, which would have mitigated the issue entirely; a question which agains opens up another labyrinth of questions.

From what we can see, he relied solely on Muhammad's followers and his wives. But how could they possibly know without the original bones and palm fronds? Islamic tradition describes these individuals persistently forgetting verses due to human error. Without an exemplar, the task of authentication would be impossible. Surely, any hardened lawyer or detective would make short work of Islam's defence of the Quran's alleged incorruptibility. As I have already proven in earlier chapters, the initial foundations of Islam and the story of Muhammad is so full of holes, it's laughable to pass off the religion with the seal of authenticity.

ONLY PROPHETS CAN CERTIFY THE QURAN

There is also the issue of Uthman's undeniable *fallibility* which ultimately would have disqualified him from asserting himself for the task of compiling a 'holy' book. According to Islamic scripture, only *Muhammad* was certified to reveal god's word, and to verify it by his own hand. As we have already learned, Muhammad swore upon an Islamic Torah as confirmation of Allah's word. Simply put, whatever *he* deemed legitimate, immediately became holy writ. As the Quran states, he is *the* final line of messengers, the seal of the prophets.

Uthman certainly was no prophet, and therefore would be wholly exempt from validating the authenticity of any Quran, especially without the original. Consequently, this would mean that a *fallible* man as Uthman must have made mistakes, thus tainting the Quran we have today. Perfection is not attributed to mankind, but to the divine - of which Muhammad claimed to be. Surely, these questions will inevitably trigger a debate to form a polarising conclusion. But the answer is quite simple, and no Muslim can deny the fact that Muhammad strictly forbade anyone, even Uthman, to add to the Quran, or take away. This is made clear in Quran 73:2-5, and indirectly reiterated in Quran 4:46 when referring to the Jews' alleged conspiracy.

More importantly, the following shows that the Quran is a fraudulent document, considering that the book was ultimately altered…

> "And the word of your Lord has been fulfilled in truth and in justice. None can alter His words, and He is the Hearing, the Knowing."
> Quran 6:115

> "And recite, [O Muhammad], what has been revealed to you of the Book of your Lord. There is no changer of His words, and never will you find in other than Him a refuge."
> Quran 18:27

> "So for their breaking of the covenant, *We cursed them* and made their hearts hard. They distort words from their [proper] usages and have forgotten a portion of that of which they were reminded…"
> Quran 5:13

If any Muslim were aware of this egregious transgression on Uthman's part, would they be willing to authenticate the Quran? I highly doubt it. At the same time, if Muslims have been worshipping a book compiled and fabricated by a man who has committed *haram* (the forbidden), would this imply that the entire Muslim nation have angered Allah and subsequently are under a curse?

Muhammad's entire mandate was to allegedly bring back the word of Allah, and to restore the Quran by way of his revelations. Again, considering that Muhammad claimed to be the 'final prophet', the continued process of restoration would be impossible after his passing. In effect, from Muhammad's own egoism, he ultimately shot the Islamic nation in the proverbial foot - no further prophets were expected to ascend to keep the word pure. It all ended with Muhammad.

What is more disturbing after analysing this tradition, it is clear that Uthman did not care whether or not he preserved *the* original Quran, but was more interested in choosing just one book, not *the* book. Regardless if it wasn't authentic, there is no mention of him ordering a full analysis. And again, I reiterate, how could he possibly know which book was *the* Quran? As we have learned, even before Muhammad's death there was still some confusion over who possessed the most accurate version of the book.

The 'book burning' traditions unequivocally demonstrate an impulsive Uthman quickly covering up the debacle with a cover story, desperate to keep order in the empire. Thus any Muslim must admit that the probability Uthman might have actually destroyed the true version revealed by Muhammad, is overwhelmingly high. And at the same time, no Muslim can deny that their beloved ancestor tarnished Islam's once alleged impeccable reputation. In effect, Uthman has left a black mark on the Islamic Ummah - for all eternity.

AN INCOHERENT BOOK

Of course, this embarrassing fiasco only demonstrates why the Quran we know today bears no semblance of chronology or context. In truth, the book is a shoddily pieced together work of literature, that bears the hallmarks of authors who were in a hurry to publish it, regardless of its inherent incoherency. It is from these facts which prove that the subsequent Islamic authors of past (Bukhari, Ibn Ishaq, Ibn Kathir, Waqidi etc) did indeed fabricate Muhammad's 'law of abrogation', to explain the persistent inconsistencies remaining in the corrupted text. The book's numerous contradictions and sudden fluctuation in tone have also puzzled secular scholars of Islam. As historians have profusely stated, the Quran is undoubtedly a loosely compiled piece of literature, lacking in veracity, and evident of conspired fabrication.

> "The book is strikingly lacking in overall structure, frequently obscure and inconsequential in both language and content, perfunctory in its linking of disparate materials, and given to the repetition of whole passages in variant versions. On this basis it can plausibly be argued that the book is the product of the belated and imperfect editing of materials from a plurality of traditions."
> 'Hagarism', Crone-Cook 1977:18,167

The Quran's lack of authenticity and inherency to self-corrupt in perpetuity, also explains why the oldest found text is again dissimilar from the version widely distributed today. In 1972, while restoration of the great mosque was being carried out in Sana'a Yemen, workers found old parchments in the loft which ultimately turned out to be the entire Quran codex, in a well-preserved condition. Seven years later, German scholar and Quran expert Dr. Gerd-r Puin from the University of Saarbrucken, began his studies on the text which revealed shocking results.

It was determined that the book was dated 705-715 A.D, which would have been in circulation around 50 years after Uthman's frantic alleged book-burning episode. Indeed, examination proved that the book was wholly dissimilar from the Cairo text we have today, and was deemed the oldest datable Quran in the world. Puin noted that the text contained immense differences with the Cairo version, as the Sana'a text's individual words could have up to 30 different meanings.

> "The text isn't as stable as it seems in the Cairo version."
> - Dr. Gerd-r Puin

Furthermore, after forensic analysis was applied, it appeared that there were actually earlier inscriptions that had been washed off, where newer verses were rewritten over them. This would most probably explain the Quran's position on abrogation. And as I have stated before, it is the *bandaid* religion.

Likewise, in 2001 another study of the Quran we have today proved so controversial, that any mention of it was banned in Islamic countries. An author writing under the pseudonym 'Christoph Luxembourg' published a book 'The Syro-Aramaic reading of the Quran', which clarified numerous problems with the Cairo text. Syro-Aramaic is regarded as the only language which can deliver the purest and intelligible translation of the book. According to academics, a quarter of the Quran contains unintelligible words. This is no surprise as the first book written in Arabic is actually *the* Quran, which was derived from Aramaic. Arabic is ultimately a new language.

Within Luxembourg's book, he made numerous comparisons which proved that the Quran has indeed been corrupted. In his findings, the Syro-Aramaic etymological translation for the word 'hijab' meaning to 'cover up', is translated to "put your belt around your hips." Likewise, perhaps the biggest gaffe in Islamic history is the term 'houris', ubiquitously known as 'virgins'. In the Quran, martyrs are apparently destined for heaven to be met with celestial nymphs. However, the Syro-Aramaic translation proves that Jihadists' death have been in vain. As the translation states…

> "We will make you comfortable under white crystal clear *grapes* (houris)."

What this entails is quite comedic, yet ultimately sad. It seems that for centuries, Muslim martyrs have foolishly died not for 72 virgins, but grapes! However, the majority of Muslims are unaware of this risible blunder, as this original text was never put into mass publication. I posit that the deliberate omissions to the original, motivated centuries of violent jihad. I doubt there would be any Muslim man on this planet today, who would die for 'grapes' instead of a celestial brothel.

While there are some fringe Muslims today who would go as far as to venerate Uthman for his initiatives, it is clear that even the early Muslims who were left with the new 'revised' version, admitted that mass quantities of the original text were left out in Uthman's Quran. Again, the following tradition demonstrates that the book burnings came so suddenly, that important traditions were wiped out overnight.

> "We used to recite a Surah which resembled in length and severity to (Sura) Bara'at (sura 9). I have, however, forgotten it with the exception of this which I remember out of it: "If there were two

valleys full of riches, for the son of Adam, he would long for a third valley, and nothing would fill the stomach of the son of Adam but dust"
Sahih Muslim 5:2286

And then there's this...

"Allah sent Muhammad with the Truth and revealed the Holy Book to him, and among what Allah revealed, was the verse of the Rajam (the stoning of married persons, male and female, who commit adultery) and we did recite this verse and understood and memorised it. Allah's Apostle did carry out the punishment of stoning and so did we after him. I am afraid that after a long time has passed, somebody will say, "By Allah, we do not find the verse of the Rajam in Allah's Book", and thus they will go astray by leaving an obligation which Allah has revealed."
Sahih Bukhari 8:82:817

As you can see, the Quran as we know today has not remained true to its original form. Nonetheless, I guarantee that if the reader were to recite my book's chapter to any Muslim, they still would not turn away from the faith. Muslims are in Islam for life. They cannot leave, and are merely in a collapsing bubble. The more they profess of Islam's alleged infallibility, their resolve eventually wavers, as the crushing weight of truth becomes intolerably burdensome.

UNDISCIPLINED DISCIPLES

Despite this obviously embarrassing debacle, there is another issue which again causes further problems for the ancient patriarchy of Islam. As the reader might be aware, the birth of Islam in Medina was formed through a strict regiment of brainwashing and recitation. The actual definition of 'Quran', is a derivative of the Arab word 'Iqra', which means to 'recite'.

As Islamic history tells, the early founders of the faith were instructed to rigorously recite, and most importantly 'memorise' the Quran in its entirety lest corruption occur. Considering the fallout of the book burning episode, there arises two conclusions which again embarrasses and actually shames the disciples of Muhammad for indolently allowing such an event to transpire.

If the true Quran was allegedly etched on every Muslim's brain, why did the corruption take place? Surely, any fervent follower of the cult would know the difference between a forgery and the authentic. But as Islamic history dictates, we see that none were able to verify the texts. In reality, the process of elimination would be simple, as any incongruous alteration would render the entire book corrupt. But if we read the Hadith, it seems that none of Muhammad's followers were able to verify the texts, resulting in Uthman quickly choosing *one* book.

This leaves us with two conclusions...

Firstly, it's highly possible that these individuals never existed at all. Art may imitate life, but the truth is far more revealing and convincing. If Aisha, Uthman, Umar, Sawda, Abu Bakr etc. all existed, surely the Hadith would have recorded these significant icons debating over the texts and their differences. At least *one* of them must have recognised the 'truth'. But as we see, all were inexplicably mute on the issue.

As I have previously outlined, the author's of Islam went as far as to fabricate an event where a sheep ate Aisha's sacred parchments. The whole backstory behind these people is flaky, at best. True history reveals intricate details of past individuals' lives, their anguish, and the struggles they faced. But the Hadith seems to paper over the inevitable frictions concerning this issue, and leads to a more simplistic solution of callously choosing *any* book to suffice.

Finally, if the disciples did exist, then they were ultimately feckless and self-involved. The fact that *none* were able to verify the original Quran, only means that the entire cult failed to memorise the entire text. If this is so, then Muhammad's incessant brainwashing tactics had failed. Thus it's fair to say that they never truly believed in the word, and only clung to Muhammad as sycophants for political reasons, while biding their time, waiting for him to die before asserting themselves for the role of caliph. After all, Uthman axiomatically couldn't have cared less about the Quran, and simply chose any book as a substitute.

This demonstrates that all supported the organisation purely for political means, seeking a way to seize power for themselves. As Islamic history dictates, my assertions are indeed correct. After Muhammad's death, major schisms broke out between the echelon, namely between Ali, Aisha and Abu Bakr. It seems that all were predominantly concerned with taking control instead of preserving the tenets of the faith. This only proves that Islam is a political animal, and that Muhammad is Islam's mascot. But these subsequent issues still do not excuse the mystery that is the Quran, and never give insight as to what the original message entailed.

WHAT WAS WRITTEN IN THE ORIGINAL QURAN?

Considering the embarrassing fiasco that is 'the Quran book burning episode', how could any Muslim truly know what was written in the original Quran? It's highly plausible that the original was far removed from the violent, psychotic manuscript we have today. Perhaps Uthman (if he actually existed), an impulsive, egomaniacal man, more interested with covering up the truth than exposing the lie, actually had ulterior motives. Maybe it was he who created *the* Islam we know today? And through *his* Quran, derives the homicidal, xenophobic and bizarre traditions known as the Hadith. Who could really know?

As I have already stated, Islam is indeed *the* 'band-aid' religion, but it's more so a mystery. And it's no surprise that Uthman acted so hastily in covering up a lie. Islam was built on lies, and will continue to be a false religion. However, a wound can only take one band-aid at a time; the rest are superfluous. The festering wound of mendacity is quickly spreading underneath its dressing. It's only a matter of time before the whole organisation becomes necrotic from the infection.

WHEN WAS ISLAM NEVER AN EXTREMIST RELIGION?

For some time, there has been a concerted effort by the leaders of the west to divorce terrorism from Islam. The liberal media and the governmental authorities have conspired together, desperately attempting to draw a distinguishable line between the fabricated 'moderate Islam' and the true tenets of the faith, disingenuously labelled as 'radical Islam'; once formerly known as 'extremist Islam'. By and large, a whole new liberal lexicon has evolved from Islamic terrorism, where those who have not yet fulfilled their obligation to Allah are dotingly labelled 'moderate Muslims'. And as the years go by, our vernacular and vocabulary might change to suit changing narratives, the problem however is that *Islamic* terrorism always remains.

Regardless that the Quran itself is a blatant manuscript for war - a document that is irremovably steeped in xenophobia - the obstinate liberal populous denies that Islam *is* a religion of hate, instead insisting that it's allegedly a 'religion of peace'. This is nothing but doublespeak. For the layman and blissfully ignorant, the seductive sales pitch of those whose agenda is more than conspicuous, is actually commendably seducing, yet ultimately nefarious. Of course, their efforts are largely in vain when the unfettered statistics regarding Islamic terrorism are becoming a burdensome stone which is slowly sinking their argument.

Since 9/11, there has been at least 25,000 Islamic terrorist attacks worldwide. Many have been on home soil, of which are becoming a monthly event. Sadly, the west has become so desensitised to Islamic terrorism in their own backyard, that it has become a way of life. By all accounts, any publicised attempts to connect Islam with terrorism is hastily downplayed as 'bigoted hate speech', worthy of global censure. Social media networks, predominantly Facebook, have become the world's new editor-in-chief, determining what is newsworthy, or propaganda. Invariably, the latter is always the truth. If the new globalist internet infrastructure isn't enough to dissuade truth-seekers, your own politicians are equally culpable in the mass coverup. As London's Muslim mayor Sadiq Khan infamously stated the faux pas, "Terrorism is just part and parcel of living in a big city."

And what's worse, is that millennials are swallowing this placating and insidious rhetoric in denial of the ominous catastrophic cataclysm which will undoubtedly destroy their over-privileged lifestyles.

Like clockwork, days after any terrorist attack, the victims' blood is speedily mopped up, wreaths are laid, candle-light vigils are held, perfunctory commemorative rock concerts are played, mosques are overzealously protected by the government, Muslims are hugged, and then it's back to work - "business as usual." Everyone is a winner, no-one is a villain. All shall sing Kumbaya ad nauseum. Terrorism is *always* swept under the carpet instead of identifying the root of the problem, which in turn perpetuates the cycle of violence. Likewise, woe to those who dare question the Muslim community, and their conspicuous failure to report their own ilk. Such a notion would constitute a hate crime, an act perceived by leftists to be worst than terrorism itself. Yet, the irony is that the Muslim community publicly and vehemently target and vilify people such as myself with impunity - as I am a direct inconvenience to them; we who speak the truth.

THE MUSLIM PROPAGANDA

There is a considerable amount of propaganda put out today which is propagated by the Muslim community in the west, as they emphatically state that Islam has always been a 'religion of peace', and never an extremist faith. Allegedly, Islam's true fundamental tenets are based on the concept of universal peace, equality and general understanding. But Muslims are not in denial, they know their religion's history - they just don't want to own up to the truth. And yet no Muhammadan can truly deny that Islam's history is steeped in violence, bloodshed and totalitarianism; and will ever be.

But besides the two-faced rhetoric which persists in deluding the uninformed, it's always been paramount and convenient for Muslims to sweep Islam's *history* under the carpet, lest further scrutiny be placed on their already suspect religion. Thus it is convenient to temporary deny recorded history to suit the liberal narrative which aids and abets the murderous cult. The current liberal discourse is one that always paints Islam as a religion of benevolence; a mystical faith which is apparently no different than Christianity. Yet anyone who will commit a modicum of time to a cursory analysis of Islamic history would see that one question remains resonant…

When was Islam never an extremist religion?

MY JIHAD?

If we are to study every facet of Islam's alleged roots, we can arrive at one conclusion - the Muhamamdan faith is unapologetically spread by the *sword*, never through peace. Jihad is the primary component which has kept the cult alive and well for over 1400 years.

And thus, Muslims are still struggling to reconcile the Quran's hateful descriptions of violence with their peaceful, civil life in the west. Over the last ten years, the deliberate obfuscation of the word 'Jihad' (struggle), has cause great confusion in the west. Over a decade ago, the misinterpretation of the word was prevalent, but not entirely inaccurate. I'm sure the reader will remember numerous news programs stating that the term was synonymous with 'holy war', where even today, liberals will cite this as a contributory factor to the fabricated 'Islamophobia'. Today, the narrative has completely changed to a more praiseworthy discourse surrounding the expression.

Who could forget the Counsel on American Islamic Relation's initiative in 2013 to deceive the public, deliberately altering the meaning to awkwardly align it with western values. According to the Hamas affiliated group, they claimed "My jihad is to stay fit despite my busy schedule", "My jihad is to build friendships across the aisle", or who could forget "My jihad is to not judge people by their cover." The glaring irony is that there should be no *struggle* for any Muslim to make friends with unbelievers, unless their religion forbade it; but Islam does.

AN EXTREMIST RELIGION

The startling fact which trumped such a farcical attempt in conning the public was when a combined poll from the Pew Research Centre reported that actually 30% or more of the Muslim world believed violent jihad was acceptable. But by C.A.I.R's contentions, jihad doesn't necessarily mean death to infidels. So why do 480,000,000 Muslims believe it's acceptable to cut off an infidel's head? Because in Islam, past is prologue, and the Quran's edicts are unquestionable. Thus there is an inherent reverence within the community to emulate their historical Muslim heroes. The truth is that jihad equates to baptism for Christians, as Bah-mitzvah is to the Jews. It's a sacred right of passage.

In fact, within their own social circles, Muslims are secretly proud of Islam's accomplishments in murdering millions. This fact cannot be denied as Islamic internet forums and bulletin boards are littered with comments celebrating the bloodshed of infidels. Even today, the events of 9/11 have created a polarising vacuum for the Muslim community, where supporters of the cause still refer to the hijackers as 'the magnificent 19', but never terrorists. And on the other hand, those who feign ignorance of their faith's doctrine continue in denial to avoid accountability, yet ultimately never denying jihad itself. I'm sure the reader has heard the usual rhetoric, "9/11 was an inside job, a false flag, it was the Jews, the Zionists etc."

The sheer apathy of Muslims over this catalytic event is staggering. Evidently so, when the American Muslim community attempted to erect an ill-timed mosque at ground zero. One need only to delicately probe the issue to see that Muslims perpetuate an atmosphere of irreverence and supremacist attitudes towards the biggest terrorist attack in U.S history. I challenge anyone to query any Muslim over the events, and you'll be met with askance looks, contempt and the odd snigger.

Undoubtedly and predictably, there will be some who will refer to the abrogated 'peaceful' verses in the Quran to seduce the public. And while it's true that a Muslim could argue that the first phase of Islamic development was historically created through peaceful intentions, a well-informed rebuttal would decimate the Muslim's argument. In my first book, I already disproved that Muhammad's initial motivations for peace were purely superficial. Unequivocally, it's evident that the 'prophet' had already set out a genocidal plan for unbelievers, and to assert his self-declared sovereignty over the world.

> "And I am planning a scheme... So give a respite to the disbelievers. Deal thou gently with them for a while."
> Quran 86:16-17

And...

> "We grant them their pleasure for a little while: in the end shall We drive them to a chastisement unrelenting."
> Quran 31:24

It is from Muhammad's own words which propelled the Islamic nation into an eternal conflict with the unbeliever. A war which will continue unabated until the whole world accepts Islam as the master faith, and *the* dominant force to rule over all lands.

> "You listen to me o' Quraysh. I swear by Allah, I will bring you slaughter!"
> Muhammad - Sirat Rasul Allah p.131 (decree before expulsion)

Hardly a statement which could be considered devoid of extremism. Of course, Muhammad's declaration of eternal war motivated the man to declare a staggering 109 genocidal verses in the Quran, which call for the brutal murder and inhuman punishment for those who reject Islam. Undoubtedly, verses which are widely considered to be 'extreme' by today's standards, but are still an intrinsic part of the Muslim faith, whose unavoidable prescription must be fulfilled. Hence why terrorism will never cease, especially when Muslims adoringly and reverently refer to these hateful edicts as the 'sword verses'.

IMMODERATE ISLAM

What is undeniable, is that Muslim advocates of 'moderate Islam' still continue to desperately downplay the faith as a mystical and peaceful religion. The poster child for moderate Islam, celebrity Doctor Oz famously stated during a PBS interview 'Faces of America', that his faith was based on the mystical elements of Islam, also drawing fascination from Islamic proverbs such as, "the reed that cries in the wilderness, because it's been cut away from the stalk that lead to its connection." As Oz has stated, his adoration for the faith derives from the Sufi movement of Islam founded Mevlana - which has historically been regarded to be the 'peaceful' interpretation of Islam. Not entirely a reformation, but more so a perversion. Ultimately, Sufism is a disingenuous form of Islam, and heavily conflicts with Muhammad's teachings. In truth, apart from its stringent accord to monotheistic principals, it bears no resemblance to fundamental Islam. Sufism conveniently, and undoubtedly, sidesteps the faith's extremist past, which is far more revealing.

Historically speaking, never has Islam been a compassionate and tolerant religion. This is not a matter of perception, but a simple fact. Of course, we can only base our analysis on official Islamic history, which was most assuredly fabricated to unify the Arab nation. The fact that early Muslims manufactured an entire false history of violence, extremism and intolerance, only proves that they revelled in butchery. If the bloodshed of alleged Islamic history was too embarrassing to admit, surely the first Muslim historians would have erased it entirely. This was not the case. Even in their wildest fantasies, genocide and the highest degree of extremism was *the* desired path to take, according to those who fabricated Muhammad, and authored the Quran-Hadith. Likewise, not only were the original authors infatuated with carnage, but the fact is that contemporary Muslims in the Arab states remain publicly and staunchly proud of their faith's deplorable history. Instead of sweeping the embarrassing truth under the carpet, true Muslims who live specifically in these regions celebrate the violence as an ordained and justified act. This method of thinking has propelled the barbarous 'Wahabi' movement.

According to what was actually recorded as official history in the annals of Islamic historical archives, it is evident that Islam was always incapable of diplomacy. Dominance has always been the primary hallmark of Muslims. Wherever the hoard spreads, their megalomania always gets the better of them. As we have quickly learned by now, there is an incessant compulsion for Islam to convert churches to mosques, to threaten the indigenous, to bully and intimidate, to demand Sharia law, and to murder their own to preserve the social structure. These are the calling cards of an extremist, intolerant society of *settlers*. Settlers who wish to colonise, not to assimilate into indigenous culture.

However, I'm sure you've heard the platitudes of the liberally aligned Muslim, "Islam respects all faiths and cultures." But how true is this statement? In actuality, the Quran leaves no wiggle room for interpretation, which explains the 1400 year history of cultural genocide at the hands of the caliphs. In truth, a Muslim cannot cherry pick verses from the Quran, and dismiss the axiomatic. The dominant message is for Muslims to impose themselves on all lands. And impose, they most certainly have.

THE GREAT MUSLIM IMPOSITION

The Hagia Sofia, once regarded as the jewel of the Bosphorus, was actually at one time a church, which was built during the Byzantine empire. However, when the Islamic Ottomans seized Turkey under Mehmet II, it was predictably converted into a mosque, erasing all traces of Christendom. The same can be said for the Dome of the Rock mosque, where Jewish influence was quickly erased after Jerusalem's fall to the Muslims. The same is happening today. In the west, Muslims are hell bent on converting churches to mosques under the pretext that there are no adequate places of worship to suit their needs. But according to Islamic history, the motivation is quite clear. Muslims *must* dominate the land they walk upon, and erase its culture, religion and national identity. Again, this signifies an example of an extremist mindset.

It is the mentality of Islam's colonial imposition which is irremovable from the Muslim psyche. A detrimental mental condition which has been solidified through Muhammad's extreme teachings and inherent xenophobia. Extremism and disrespect go hand in hand. It is by extremism and intolerance that Islam flourished. Let's face it, Islam is not a seductive religion, it has to be forced down the throats of its subordinates. Not even the early Muslims could fully swallow the poison Muhammad was selling, as they periodically refrained from their leader's genocidal teachings.

> "Killing has been prescribed for you while it is hateful to you. But perhaps you hate a thing and it is good for you; and perhaps you love a thing and it is bad for you."
> Quran 2:216

I challenge any Muslim reading this to come up with one example in history where the Islamic nation has extended the olive branch to the unbeliever, without taking a position of superiority. Simply put, such an event has never occurred. Neither has diplomacy or tolerance been openly witnessed within the confines of the faith. By coining the terms 'murtad' (apostate) and 'munafiq' (hypocrite), Muhammad created a cultural vacuum where Muslims were implored to spy on each other; to observe and report. For anyone who refuses to rat on their own, their salvation is deemed questionable. This is typical of cults who use fear, superstition and paranoia to keep followers in line. Of course, if Islam truly was a peaceful religion, these practices would not exist. Love and harmony would organically flow through the Ummah, and all the world would rush to *revert* back to Islam.

Undeniably, the term 'apostate' has become a political weapon to filter out tourists and political liabilities, and in turn has lead to the plaguing issue of 'honour killings'. The honour killing phenomenon is now officially on the rise in the west, even surpassing the middle-east statistically. This is happening because Muslims are inevitably and increasingly becoming westernised, much to the chagrin of their fundamental, orthodox parents. Of course, it takes a good spell of rigorous Islamic indoctrination, guilting, bullying, or even threats of death to bring them back to the faith. And this is where radicalisation takes hold of their lives, and the lives of others who interact with them. When all else fails, the honour killing route is always perceived to be god's divine judgment. This is not a baseless assertion, but the hard facts.

FANATICAL AND FATALISTIC

It seems that ritualistic indoctrination spans through all age groups in Islam, as not even Muslim children are impervious to Islam's ritualistic brainwashing, which comes in the form of the 'Qirat', a.k.a Quran recitation school. While your own western children are happily exposed to colourful cartoons, fun learning games, or lessons on morality via nursery rhymes, Muslim children waste their precious years being subjected to rigorous memorisation of the *entire* Quran. There is a pervasive stigma in the Muslim community where shame is cast on those who fail to recite the Quran. In fact, since Muhammad laid the foundations of compulsion, an honorary title is given to those who can recite the entire book, word by word. Such people are revered as 'Hafiz'. Muslim mother's especially are known to drive their children to obtain this useless title, and thus we have seen the rise of Muslim child abuse at the hands of cowardly parents. Brutal punishment is always prescribed for innocent Muslim children who rightfully have no interest in parroting inane verses, created by a narcissistic, child molesting dwarf.

In 2017, a Welsh Muslim mother was jailed after beating her son to death "like a dog", and subsequently burning his corpse in a fit of rage - to hide the shame. Not her shame, but the fact that the boy had offended Allah due to not being able to memorise the Quran. As reports state, the child was subjected to a steady progression of brutal punishment applied by the mother, stemming from this issue. According to the police, the young boy received systematic corporal punishment over weeks, where authorities became somewhat aware when teachers were suspicious that the child could no longer use his right hand to write, thus resorting to the left. In truth, our governments failed to act, and the boy's blood is on the crown's hands. To add insult to injury, due to our liberal governments' inability to pass effective judgment, she will be eligible for parole in only 17 years. Over fifty years ago, she would have received the death penalty for murdering a child - regardless if she was a Muslim.

But as much as Muslims and their organisations will attempt to downplay these crimes, the fact is that such atrocities will continue, so long as the Quran propagates extremism throughout the community. In 2009, in an ironic twist of fate, Muzzammil Hassan, who was the founder of an upstate New York Muslim TV station, which was actively dedicated to combating negative Muslim stereotypes, predictably fell back into fundamental Islam by committing the unthinkable. Hassan's wife had filed for divorce after facing years of domestic abuse at the hands of her husband. Hassan himself could have defied negative Muslim stereotypes to take the higher ground, but alas the man fell short of virtue. The husband was charged and sentenced for decapitating his wife, after stabbing her 40 times to death, in the face, back and chest.

Not surprisingly, while the aforementioned are not to be pardoned, their crimes only reflect back on Islamic extremist teachings. These are not isolated incidents. On the contrary! There are literally hundreds of new stories each day which exemplify Muslim violence, all conforming to Islam; an ancient culture of barbarism. After all it was Muhammad who set the tone for extremist thought, when he said that Muslims' homes should be burned down if anyone fails to attend the mosque to recite the Quran. The same would also apply to infidels, or equally women who go astray.

> Narrated Abu Huraira: The Prophet said, "No prayer is harder for the hypocrites than the Fajr and the 'Isha' prayers and if they knew the reward for these prayers at their respective times, they would certainly present themselves (in the mosques) even if they had to crawl." The Prophet added, "Certainly I decided to order the Mu'adh-dhin (call-maker) to pronounce Iqama and order a man to lead the prayer and then take a fire flame to burn all those who had not left their houses so far for the prayer along with their houses."
> Sahih Bukhari 1:11:626

Yet, I can not help but recount Churchill's infamous words of wisdom in his unfettered description of the cult.

"How dreadful are the curses which Mohammedanism lays on its votaries! Besides the *fanatical frenzy*, which is as dangerous in a man as hydrophobia in a dog, there is this *fearful fatalistic apathy.*"

Thus is the problem with Islam. It's the inherent fatalistic attitude which it harbours that perpetuates extremism in all forms. Yet it's ironic that western governments are now capitulating from labelling such lunatics who burn their own children, or decapitate their wives as extremists, and will instead bestow the stereotype solely on critics of Islam. In a world gone mad, people like myself are regarded as the neo-extremists and terrorists; those who dare to say the obvious.

In actuality, Muslim austerity itself is a form of cultural and social terrorism. Fear and punishment comes in many forms. In truth, honour killings serve to be a warning for those who venture beyond the confines of Islam, or even dare to have fun and independence from dogmatism. As former Ayatollah Khomeini infamously stated...

> "Allah did not create man so that he could have fun. The aim of creation was for mankind to be put to the test through hardship and prayer. An Islamic regime must be serious in every field. There are no jokes in Islam. There is no humor in Islam. There is no fun in Islam. There can be no fun and joy in whatever is serious. ..."
> - Political thought and legacy of Khomeini

THE APARTHEID RELIGION

If anyone still perceives Islam *not* to be an extremist ideology, they must be delusional. Throughout the history of the west, no foreign migrant has ever instituted the dreaded 'no-go zone', only except Muslims. To play devil's advocate however, how can Muslim migrants be blamed for their attitudes, when the Quran prescribes the most extreme form of xenophobia regarding unbelievers? In the eyes of a Muslim, non-Muslims are dirty, of the devil, and will corrupt anyone with their evil. Naturally, to justify their hermetic lifestyles and to cast off criticism and suspicion from their hosts, the ubiquitous 'Islamophobia' term has been weaponised in hopes of silencing critics. The radical left has revelled in this fabricated term, but ironically fails to recognise that the fundamental tenets of Islam are steeped in

'Christophobia' and 'Jewophobia'. Of course, it has become more acceptable and popular to criticise Jews and Christians. After all, such peoples lack the propensity to lash out in acts of terror.

Furthermore, if Islam allegedly has never been an extremist culture, then why do Muslims feel compelled today to remove the cross everywhere they go? Naturally, this intolerant and extremist attitude over an innocuous religious symbol is based on Islamic tradition. The Islamic 'Pact of Umar' is perhaps the most extremist form of legislation that was ever created in history, identical to the Nazi regime's own mandates and Nuremberg laws. It is this piece of legislation which has been followed in perpetuity, which has given rise to the anti-Christian sentiment throughout the Muslim community in the west. According to the Pact, no cross should ever be erected in Muslim lands, and all unbelievers must take a position of inferiority to the Ummah.

This methodology has provoked numerous instances of Muslim gangs patrolling the U.K and now particularly Germany. These Islamic vigilante groups terrorise 'moderate' Muslim citizens on the streets for simply enjoying the western lifestyle, all according to their brand of Quranic justice. In reality, these overzealous firebrands are imitating the age old tradition of the 'Mutaween', the Islamic religious police which exist today predominantly in Saudi Arabia, Iran and Pakistan. The reader may ask the question, what gives Muslim migrants the right to dictate how the indigenous should behave? Quite simply, the Quran teaches that if a Muslim occupies any piece of land, it becomes 'Islamic' by default, and the ground immediately becomes hallowed, reclaimed for the caliphate.

Thus according to Muslims living in Tower Hamlets London, Luton, Bradford and throughout the EU, the soil they reside upon apparently belongs to Allah.

> Thauban reported that Allah's Messenger said: "Allah drew the ends of the world near one another for my sake. And I have seen its eastern and western ends. *And the dominion of my Ummah would reach those ends which have been drawn near me and I have been granted the red and the white treasure* and I begged my Lord for my Ummah that it should not be destroyed because of famine, nor be dominated by an enemy who is not amongst them to take their lives and destroy them root and branch, and my Lord said: Muhammad, whenever I make a decision, there is none to change it. I grant you for your Ummah that it would not be destroyed by famine and it would not be dominated by an enemy who would not be amongst it and would take their lives and destroy them root and branch even if all the people from the different parts of the world join hands together (for this purpose), but it would be from amongst them, viz. your Ummah, that some people would kill the others or imprison the others."
> Sahih Muslim 2889

"It is He who has sent His Messenger with guidance and the religion of truth *to manifest it over all religion,*

although they who associate others with Allah dislike it."
Quran 9:33

This explains why Muslim migration has exponentially increased ten-fold within only a few years. Muslims now have a new territory to breed on. A caliphate is on the rise, steeped in extremism and apartheid values.

Furthermore, the extremist Pact of Umar's ordinances are entirely legitimised by the Quran, which orders that Muslims stringently separate themselves from the unbeliever, at all costs. Even in death, no Muslim is permitted to be buried next to an infidel or apostate. And lest we forget, Muhammad strictly forbade crying and emotion at funerals; hallmarks of an extremist cult.

> 'Abdullah b. 'Umar reported that Hafsa wept for 'Umar (when he was about to die). He ('Umar) said: "Be quiet, my daughter. Don't you know that the Messenger of Allah had said:" The deceased is punished because of his family's weeping over the death?"
> Sahih Muslim 927

Consequently, the west has unnecessarily and obsequiously complied to Islamic intimidation by designating Islamic graveyards, completely separating Muslims from Christians, Jews, Sihks, Buddhists etc. To cut oneself off from the greater public should be considered as an extremist act. Yet our governments defend the undercurrent of

Islamic apartheid driven narrative, citing religious freedom while playing the 'Islamophobia' card.

ISLAM IS ISLAM - A GENOCIDAL CULT

I'm sure you've heard most Muslim leaders repetitiously state the ubiquitous platitude, "the terrorists have hijacked our religion." This assertion is an exercise in futility, as not all Muslims agree. As Turkish President Recep Erdogan so eloquently corrected this growing rhetoric…

"These descriptions are very ugly, it is offensive and an insult to our religion. There is no moderate or immoderate Islam. Islam is Islam and that's it."

Let's be honest, Erdogan is hardly someone who is ill-informed about the precepts of the faith. In recent times, Turkey has become a neoconservative, dictatorial, Sharia compliant state through a resurgence of Islamic values, perpetrated by Erdogan. If there is no 'moderate Islam', and if extremism propagates throughout the Islamic community, surely we must deduce that Islam is certainly an extremist religion. Perhaps we should consider Gaza and the West Bank. Both are theocratic regions which implore violence, encourage martyrdom, all for a lost cause. Palestinians are notorious for naming streets after terrorists, and mothers macabrely celebrate their sons deaths, implying that they have been wedded to 72 brides in heaven. The authorities hold parades, where Muslim children are decorated with artificial suicide-bomber vests, while carrying plastic toy Qassam rockets, screaming "death to the west, death to Israel!" Again, all signs of an extremist society hell-bent on its own self-destruction.

And it is through Palestine's adoption of fundamental Islamic principals, of which are unavoidably steeped in extremist thought, that has kept them in a state of regression. These two theocratically controlled areas are so focused on wiping Israel off the face of the planet, albeit with sticks and stones, they've missed the bigger picture - they've ruined any chance of their nations ever progressing.

While the radical left will wince at this remark, in truth, no other religion in history has created more terrorist organisations like Islam has. The faith's tenets have an inherent knack of breeding the worst form of human being. And by that regard, Islam is nothing more than a terrorist factory. For example, both Hamas and Iran's own constitutional preambles call for a perpetual jihad and the annihilation of Israel. These are the obscure facts which the media seldom reports, but are freely accessibly to read.

Under the Iranian constitutional charter 'Ideological army', the regimes states…

> "In the formation and equipping of the country's defence forces, due attention must be paid to faith and ideology as the basic criteria. Accordingly, the Army of the Islamic Republic of Iran and the Islamic Revolutionary Guards Corps are to be organized in conformity with this goal, and they will be responsible not only for guarding and preserving the frontiers of the country, but also for fulfilling the ideological mission of jihad in God's way; that is, extending the sovereignty of God's law throughout the world (this is in accordance with the Koranic verse "Prepare against them whatever force

you are able to muster, and strings of horses, striking fear into the enemy of God and your enemy, and others besides them" [8:60])."

Similarly, the 'Covenant of the Hamas' theocratic charter echoes the same genocidal tone...

"The day that enemies usurp part of Moslem land, Jihad becomes the individual duty of every Moslem. In face of the Jews' usurpation of Palestine, it is compulsory that the banner of Jihad be raised. To do this requires the diffusion of Islamic consciousness among the masses, both on the regional, Arab and Islamic levels. It is necessary to instil the spirit of Jihad in the heart of the nation so that they would confront the enemies and join the ranks of the fighters."

And...

"Moreover, if the links have been distant from each other and if obstacles, placed by those who are the lackeys of Zionism in the way of the fighters obstructed the continuation of the struggle, the Islamic Resistance Movement aspires to the realisation of Allah's promise, no matter how long that should take. The Prophet, Allah bless him and grant him salvation, has said:

"The Day of Judgement will not come about until Moslems fight the Jews (killing the Jews), when the Jew will hide behind stones and trees. The stones and trees will say O Moslems, O Abdulla, there is a Jew behind me, come and kill him. Only the Gharkad tree, (evidently a certain kind of tree) would not do that because it is one of the trees of the Jews." (related by al-Bukhari and Moslem)."

Littered throughout the entire Hamas manuscript are dozens of anti-semitic edicts which would make a reasonably-minded person's stomach churn. But what can we expect from a cult which has imbibed the narcissistic poison of their prophet.

Of course, in any extremist society, religion or creed, the issue of genocide is always a side-effect of a cult-like mentality. Islam and mass-murder have proven to share an incestuous relationship. As I demonstrated in my first book, the aftermath of Islamic conquest has staggeringly amounted to an estimated body count of 270,000,000 non-Muslims over a millennia years. This obscene figure is not even counting the daily beheadings in Saudi Arabia, where such morbid and grotesque spectacles are watched upon as sport, instead of punishment.

For anyone to deny that Islam defines extremist thought, there is obviously an inherent unwillingness to face the truth. Not even the liberal community can deny these facts, but instead have invested a considerable amount of time embellishing the gory details of Islamic doctrine and its sordid past. For someone like myself who thrives on truth and expects nothing less than honesty, to dissemble over Islam's obvious links to terrorism is a clear indictment on anyone who would dare advocate the faith.

COMING SOON...

QUESTIONS THAT
ISLAM
CAN'T ANSWER
VOLUME TWO

I ASK THE TOUGH QUESTIONS ABOUT...

'ALLAH'

NOTES

Printed in Great Britain
by Amazon